REALITY TELEVISION

CONTRACTS

How to Negotiate the Best Deal

PAUL BATTISTA AND HAYLEY HUGHES

ALLWORTH PRESS
NEW YORK

Allworth Press books may be purchased in bulk at special discounts for sales promotion, corporate gifts, fund-raising, or educational purposes. Special editions can also be created to specifications. For details, contact the Special Sales Department, Allworth Press, 307 West 36th Street, 11th Floor, New York, NY 10018 or info@skyhorsepublishing.com.

19 18 17 16 15   5 4 3 2 1

Published by Allworth Press, an imprint of Skyhorse Publishing, Inc.
307 West 36th Street, 11th Floor, New York, NY 10018.

Allworth Press® is a registered trademark of Skyhorse Publishing, Inc.®, a Delaware corporation.

www.allworth.com

Cover and interior design by Mary Belibasakis.

Library of Congress Cataloging-in-Publication Data is available on file.

Print ISBN: 978-1-621-53-486-0
Ebook ISBN: 978-1-62153-496-9

Printed in the United States of America.

Contents

Acknowledgments   v

Introduction   1

PART I:

Background of Reality Television   3

   1. *Very Brief History of Reality Television*   5
   2. *"Standard" / "Boilerplate" Terms*   11

PART II:

Development   23

   3. *Talent Attachment Agreement*   25
      Deal Point Checklist   46
   4. *Collaboration Agreement Between Two Production Companies*   49
      Deal Point Checklist   66

PART III:

Production   67

   5. *Participant Agreement Between a Production Company and*
      an On-Air Participant   69
   6. *On-Air Talent Agreement Between a Production Company and "Talent"*   102
      Deal Point Checklist   143
   7. *Production Services Agreement*   145
      Deal Point Checklist   173
   8. *Location Agreement*   174
      Deal Point Checklist   181

Index   183

Acknowledgments

PAUL BATTISTA

I would like to acknowledge and thank my wife, Leah, for her continuous support and encouragement. I would also like to thank Tad Crawford at Allworth Press for his guidance and vision in shaping the book.

HAYLEY HUGHES

I would like to thank my mama and best friend, Karen, for loving me unconditionally—I love you to the moon and back. I would also like to thank Jimmy for loving me exactly how I am but always pushing me to be a better version of myself—I'm forever yours, faithfully. Finally, to Paul, thank you for having the brilliant idea to write this book.

that are used to provide the foundation and structure of the participants' relationships are developing with it. Therefore, we believe this dialogue is important for the development of the terms found in these agreements.

The contracts that have developed into the primary ones used in reality television have their roots in the contracts that have been used in the development, production, and broadcast of other television genres, for example, sitcoms, dramas, and game shows. However, much of the language specific to reality television is the result of the innovation and imagination of the participants in the process, including the attorneys engaged to draft the contracts. Our comments and guidance regarding the terms in this book are based on our years of experience counseling clients in the development, production, and broadcast of their reality television shows. However, it must be noted that the television industry changes quickly, the law is dynamic and is changing daily, and the legal information presented at the date of publication of this book will not be updated until a subsequent edition is published. Legal information presented in the book is generally based on federal law, California state law, and New York state law, and the facts specific to any situation in which the reader may find himself or herself will be unique and different from the facts presented in this book, thereby making any parallel conclusions to the reader's specific circumstances inaccurate. In addition, the reader may be subject to laws different from the federal and state laws presented in this book.

THEREFORE, WE MUST POINT OUT THAT THE READER SHOULD NOT RELY ON THE LEGAL INFORMATION PRESENTED IN THIS BOOK TO ANSWER HIS OR HER SPECIFIC LEGAL QUESTIONS NOR RELY ON THE ACCURACY OF SUCH INFORMATION. RATHER, THE READER SHOULD ENGAGE THE SERVICES OF QUALIFIED, EXPERIENCED LEGAL COUNSEL.

PART I:

*Background of Reality
Television*

1

Very Brief History of Reality Television

The history of the current forms of reality television is not very deep; it can be traced back to the year 2000, when the show *Survivor* aired. The mainstream success of that show spurred networks to add reality television to its broadcast offerings. As of 2015, reality television programs are aired on over fifty different channels. However, reality television had been slowly developing for a number of years before *Survivor* brought the genre to the mainstream. The format of capturing "real" people in "real" circumstances dates back to the 1940s and 1950s. Perhaps two of the more successful shows during that time frame were *Candid Camera* in the 1940s and *Queen for a Day* in the 1950s. Both shows featured real people in circumstances in which they were themselves, revealing who they were either through their actions or through answers to questions, and thereby creating drama, suspense, or comedy from the results. Both shows generated record amounts of advertising dollars and were aired for many years. There also were successful reality-based shows on television in the 1960s and 1970s, for example: *This Is Your Life*, *Mutual of Omaha's Wild Kingdom*, *Seven Up!*, *An American Family*, *The Undersea World of Jacques Cousteau*, and *Family*.

This is an appropriate place to address the definition of the genre of reality television as applied in this book. The agreements commented on in this book are applicable to the reality television genres *other than* talk shows (for example, *The View*), traditional game shows (for example, *The Price Is Right*), and news programs (for example, *Face the Nation*). The agreements provided *are* a basic format used in reality based programs in sub-genres such as "competition" shows (for example, *The Apprentice*), "makeover/improvement" shows (for example, *The Biggest Loser* and *Restaurant: Impossible*), "hidden camera" shows (for example, *Punk'd*), and "soap opera" shows (*The Real World, The Osbournes, Keeping Up With The Kardashians, Little Couple,* and *The Real Housewives*). The agreements are basic and provide a framework for understanding what is encompassed in reality-based contracts, but each show has its own unique rules and issues that require an attorney to draft language that is specific to each show. The attorney often works closely with the producers of the show to understand and to incorporate the specific language required for each show.

Reality television continued its growth in the 1980s, when a new reality genre emerged; the "professional" procedural genre. *Cops* debuted and immediately became a hit show that has aired continuously for over twenty-five years. The show is based on camera crews following police officers doing their jobs, including interacting with and apprehending criminals. *The Real World* debuted in 1992 and had broadcast its thirtieth season by 2015. This show, reportedly modeled after the PBS series *An American Family*, is credited with starting the genre of placing strangers together to live and interact while the cameras capture everything that happens. Reality television was definitely growing, but it wasn't until the late 1990s and early 2000s that it developed beyond a niche genre to capture a large, mainstream audience. Successful shows were no longer just aired on niche cable channels but were found on the largest top networks such as CBS, NBC, ABC, and Fox. Early successful shows included *Survivor, Big Brother, The Amazing*

Race, and *American Idol*, which were quickly followed by *The Biggest Loser, The Apprentice, Dancing With the Stars, America's Got Talent, Last Comic Standing*, and *Hell's Kitchen*. It should be noted that although most reality shows are not aired on one of the big four networks (CBS, NBC, ABC, and Fox), there are many more opportunities to bring a reality show to one of the other approximately forty-five networks that air reality shows. This is simply because there are more of these channels and also because a show doesn't need to reach a large, mainstream audience. The big four networks certainly have aired successful reality shows since 2000, but *each* network also has aired at least thirty reality shows in that time that have not lasted more than one season. It is very difficult to secure a deal with any network to produce and air a show, and it is even more difficult to develop, produce, and air a reality show that will last more than one season.

The networks that are not one of the big four networks have also produced and aired successful reality shows since the beginning of 2000. For example, A&E network has aired *Duck Dynasty*, Bravo network has aired *The Real Housewives*, E! Network has aired *Keeping Up with the Kardashians*, MTV has aired *The Real World* and *Jersey Shore*, UPN has aired *America's Top Model*, and TLC network has aired *Jon and Kate Plus 8*. These networks have also aired hundreds of other reality programs since 2000. For all of the networks, there are thousands of reality programs that are developed for every one show that is aired, so development is where much of the reality television work occurs for producers and their attorneys.

THE PLAYERS

The process of developing a reality television show begins with developing an idea. Ideas are developed by producers into treatments, loglines, one-sheets, episode summaries, season structures, and often the production of a sizzle reel. Loglines are a one- or two-sentence pitch of the show, and treatments are a four- to ten page detailed description of the elements that comprise a show. A one-sheet is a one- to two-page summary of the show, and the episode summaries and season structures are, as their names indicate, a summary of each episode of the show and the main developments of a season. A sizzle reel is a short, edited presentation of a show that may focus on the show elements, the talent involved, other similar shows, edited "scenes," or a combination of these elements.

Rarely, if ever, do producers pitch or present shows for which they have not written at least a one-sheet, treatment, and logline. Often it is asked what is the best way to legally protect the elements of a reality television show. This is a topic that could be the subject of a complete separate book, so it will not be discussed in detail here. Suffice it to say that it is wise to register all written documents with the United States Copyright Office, and within those written documents to list and describe as many of the specific elements that make up the reality show, also describing the unique ways the specific elements interact.

It is important to briefly describe the process of developing a reality television program, and to also identify the primary "players" involved. Producers, often using their own production companies, work together to develop a reality television program which requires a "collaboration agreement." A producer very often attaches talent to a reality television program at the beginning of the development process, which also requires the negotiation of and entering into a "talent attachment agreement." The talent could be a local veterinarian, an exterminator, an interesting personality, and maybe even a recognizable person from television or movies, although successfully attaching a celebrity is more likely to happen for an established, successful reality television producer or production company than someone developing his or her first reality show.

Once a producer has created or engaged others to create a reality show's logline, treatment, one-sheet, signed talent attachment agreements, and often a completed sizzle reel, he or she is ready to bring the show to third parties in the hopes of moving the show to a successful realization. There is not one path that a reality show follows to reach a successful resolution. The most common next step is for a producer to approach established, successful production companies to pitch the show to those companies. It is not common for a producer without a track record of successful reality television shows to directly approach and convince a network to buy or produce a reality television show, although it has happened. Examples of successful reality television production companies include Bunim/Murray Productions, Eyeworks, Shed Media, T Group Productions, 51 Minds, and Pilgrim Studios. There are also other production companies that may not be as large or successful as the latter companies, but nevertheless are producing reality television content that is currently airing on networks.

If a production company is interested in a show, the producer will negotiate and enter a "shopping agreement," a "talent attachment agreement" (for producer services), or a "collaboration agreement" with the production company. The production company will then seek the interest of a network, also known as "the people who write checks." Examples of networks include NBC, CBS, MTV, Bravo, and Animal Planet. The goal is to obtain an order for a minimum of number of episodes of the show by a network, the terms of such order to be found in a "production service agreement." This brief summary of the parties involved leaves out one of the most important groups of "people who write checks," that is, the advertisers who pay the networks to place commercial ads during the airing of the reality television show. Producers do not have direct contact with the advertisers, but it is the ability of the producer to create and attach himself or herself to a reality television show that is aired by a network—and which then becomes a "hit" show—that earns large amounts of advertising revenue that will affect the ability of the producer to create more shows and to have more "leverage" to obtain more favorable terms in subsequent reality television agreements. The amount of leverage, or lack of leverage, that a party has to demand more favorable terms is noted throughout the comments to the agreements in this book.

Two other groups of individuals that a producer works with, once a show is ordered for production, are reality show "participants" and "on-air talent." Participants are the people who have little or no experience appearing on television but who audition to be a participant or contestant on a reality television show. Participants basically have no leverage in the negotiating process, and they are required to sign a lengthy "participant agreement" in which they consent to give the producers many wide-ranging rights. For example, they agree that the producers have the right to invade the participant's privacy, the right to reveal personal and defamatory information, and the right to engage in other actions such as providing the participant misrepresentations, placing the participant in hazardous circumstances, and many other similar terms. It should be noted that cast members of the MTV reality show *The Jersey Shore*, and cast members of other hit reality television shows, signed participant agreements containing similar language. Once their shows became hit shows, however, their leverage increased and they were able to renegotiate the terms of their participation. It should also be noted that since the terms of a participant agreement are rarely subject to negotiation—that is, they are basically take-it-or-leave-it agreements—a "Deal Point" checklist has not been included at the end of Chapter 5. "On-air talent agreements" are with individuals who have a certain talent or expertise that a producer wants to add to a show, and they are usually with individuals who have television experience or a special talent that relates to a specific reality show. For example, the host of *Dancing with the Stars* will most likely have experience in television, and a judge on the show will most likely have experience as a successful dancer and choreographer.

2

"Standard" / "Boilerplate" Terms

Standard terms, also called "boilerplate" terms, are found in reality television contracts. Although these terms are found in all properly drafted contracts, each contract defines each term using slightly different language and each contract will also address different issues under the same heading in each different contract. Therefore, the length of each paragraph under each heading will vary from as brief as a sentence or two in length in a "shopping agreement" to multiple pages in length in a "production services agreement." For example; the results and proceeds paragraph could be one sentence stating that all work is a "work-for-hire" owned by the producer. On the other hand, it could be multiple pages in which the specific rights that are owned are named and defined, in addition to addressing many other issues. It is common to have shorter paragraphs of standard terms in short form agreements that run from two to ten pages in length. Conversely, agreements such as those with television networks that are fifty to one hundred pages in length contain standard terms and provisions paragraphs that are very detailed, often covering multiple pages.

The standard terms and provisions are areas of negotiation and drafting that are primarily the responsibility of the attorney representing each party. It is not uncommon for an established reality television individual to be represented by an agent, a manager, and an attorney, each providing a different service. It is also not uncommon for established reality television production companies and networks to be represented by business executives and business affairs individuals. Agents, managers, and business executives focus primarily on the details of the show and the basic deal terms of an agreement; for example, the budget, the cast, the services to be provided, the payments for the services and the rights provided, and each party's on-screen credit. Attorneys and business affairs individuals are expected to understand the legal language in "standard"/"boilerplate" language, and it is their job to negotiate and redraft these terms for their clients. It should be noted that attorneys and business affairs executives often comment on and redraft language regarding the terms that agents, managers and business executives negotiate. Further, feedback from agents, managers, and business executives regarding "boilerplate" language is welcomed by attorneys and business affairs individuals, but most often agents, managers, and executives are happy to leave this task to the attorneys and business affair individuals. Therefore, it is important for attorneys and business affairs people to study and know the specific language "boilerplate" paragraphs in order to be able to redraft such language to their clients' benefit. However, for efficiency and clarity, the specific language of these "boilerplate" terms is omitted here and replaced with a brief definition of each term and a brief explanation of some of the issues that one should be aware of when negotiating and redrafting such terms.

1) <u>Results and Proceeds/Grant of Rights/Rights</u>: These terms provide language to define the party who owns the rights to the show. Results and Proceeds address the rights that exist when an individual provides services in creating a show. For example, a producer may agree to provide work polishing the episodes of the show—that is, rewriting episodes, assisting in producing a sizzle reel, and otherwise providing services to the development, production, and sale of the show. The language in this paragraph defines those rights and, crucially, states which

party owns such rights. The Grant of Rights is language that will specify the rights that each party holds to the show and specifically state that all of those rights are transferred (or will be transferred upon sale or license of the show in the future) to another party. The Rights are often specifically defined according to each medium so there is clarity of the rights that are subject to transfer. The language defining such rights often includes a statement preceding the definitions of the rights that "such 'Rights' include all rights to the show, including, but not limited to, the following," thereafter defining each right in detail.

The importance of having these terms in a reality television contract can't be overemphasized. Ownership of the intellectual property and all other rights to a show is required to license and sell the show and also to determine which parties are necessary and which parties are expendable. That is, no show can be licensed or sold without the owner(s) of the rights to the show transferring such rights to the licensee or purchaser. As such, the owner of the rights has a leverage position to insist that he or she be included in the licensing or sale of the show, and also has a stronger position to negotiate more favorable terms in negotiations.

2) <u>Representations and Warranties</u>: The parties to an agreement will provide assurances that certain statements that are included in this paragraph are true. For example, individuals *providing services* or rights to a show will state that he or she: can enter the agreement without violating any third party's rights, has not entered into a previous agreement that would interfere with providing services or transferring rights to the other party, and is providing material that is original and/or completely owned by the individual and will not violate any right of any other party. Individuals and companies *transferring rights* of the show to a third party—for example, transferring copyright and trademark rights—also promise that they in fact own all of the rights that are transferred and that there are no liens or any rights existing that can or will interfere with the rights that are provided to the third

party. An example of a previous action that would violate these terms is if the party providing services to the show had previously signed an agreement with a different company promising to provide *exclusive* producing services to that company or promising to give that company the first the right of negotiation to acquire or develop the show—that is, the right to acquire or develop the show before any other third party. It would not be cost-efficient or practical for each party to an agreement to thoroughly investigate whether there was a *previous* agreement entered that would interfere with the terms of the agreement they are entering, so instead, each party in effect promises in the representations and warranties that there are no hidden problems that could later emerge to frustrate the intent of their current agreement.

3) <u>Indemnification</u>: These terms provide a remedy if one of the "representations and warranties" promised by a party is later violated, which also is called a "breach." If a representation or warranty is later breached, then the party who is responsible for such breach promises to indemnify the other party or parties in the contract. "Indemnify" is a legal term that basically means the breaching party will have to pay the other party for any and all claims, demands, suits, liabilities, losses, costs, expenses, damages, or recoveries suffered, made, incurred, or assumed by reason of or arising out of any breach of any agreement, warranty, and/or representation made by the party to the agreement.

For example, if the creator of a reality show signed an agreement to allow a production company to develop the show and subsequently signed an agreement with a different production company to develop the same show, then clearly the creator has entered into a previous agreement that would interfere with providing services or transferring rights to the second production company. The creator has breached his, her, or its representations and warranties and will be responsible to pay the second production company for losses, costs, expenses, etc. that come from that breach. Often contracts require insurance be obtained and carried regarding reality shows, which may cover the payments required from the promise to indemnify the other party for violating representations and warranties.

4) <u>Assignment</u>: The party that obtains the ownership to the show—that is, obtains the Results and Proceeds, Grant of Rights, and Rights—will want and need the right to assign such rights to third parties. "Assign" and "assignment" are legal terms for transfer. This paragraph will clearly state that the party that has the rights can assign, transfer, or license any and all rights to any third party without the consent or approval of anyone. The party that allows assignment wants to add that if such assignment occurs then the new party must agree to accept all of the terms originally agreed to and, further, the party to the agreement agrees to remain secondarily liable for the obligations in the agreement. This prevents the transferring party from assigning the rights to a third party who could later refuse to comply with the terms originally agreed to; for example, payments or on-screen credit, or from transferring the rights to an unreliable third party.

5) <u>Remedies</u>: If one of the parties to the agreement doesn't comply with the terms—that is, breaches the agreement—then this paragraph provides terms regarding the rights of each party. A common legal "remedy" is that one party is required to pay the other party money for damages that arise from a breach. However, there are other remedies that do not require payment of money, such as an injunction or specific performance. These remedies are called "equitable remedies." An injunction is an equitable remedy that prohibits someone from taking a specific action. Specific performance is an equitable remedy that requires a party to do a specific action. If a network acquired, developed, and aired a reality show that became successful, it is not hard to imagine the losses involved for the network if it breached an agreement regarding the show and the aggrieved party were able to obtain an injunction prohibiting the network from airing the show. Because of the power of equitable remedies, the party obtaining the show's rights in the agreement requires the other party to allow equitable

If an event of force majeure occurs, then the service provider's engagement, services, and the accrual of compensation is deemed automatically suspended for the duration of such force majeure event. The service provider's attorney will want to include language that ensures that the service provider is only suspended from work during a force majeure event if individuals on the project with the same or lesser job title are also suspended. An issue the attorneys will want to address is whether or not the service provider is allowed to provide service to a third party during the force majeure event, and if so, what the service provider's responsibilities to return are if called back by the employer. Once a force majeure event suspends services, it is customary that it continues until the employer provides the service provider notice to return to work. If the event continues past a specified time limit, often four weeks, then the employer usually has the right to terminate the agreement.

8) <u>Morals</u>: Most reality television contracts do not contain a "morals" clause. A morals clause is when an employer requires a service provider to agree to conduct himself or herself in a certain manner, both on and off the set, or risk termination from the show. The language can be innocuous, wherein the employer requires the service provider to act in a businesslike manner at all times while rendering services. As would be expected, most service providers do not find the latter terms disagreeable. Sometimes an employer will add language stating that if the service provider is convicted of a felony or any crime involving substance abuse, child abuse, domestic abuse and/or moral turpitude, then the employer can terminate the agreement. Most service providers do not have an issue agreeing to the latter terms, but it certainly depends. The following language is often where service providers become reluctant to agree to "morals" language because of the ambiguous nature of the language used. For example, sometimes an employer will want the right to terminate the agreement if the service provider "fails to conduct himself or herself with due regard to

public conventions and morals, or does any act or fails to do any act, which act or omission will be or may hold (the service provider) up to public contempt or ridicule or which will or may otherwise tend to adversely affect public acceptance of the reality television show." It is clear that this language is ambiguous and leaves much room for interpretation and litigation. Nevertheless, larger production companies and certainly networks most often will require on-camera talent to agree to a morals clause.

9) <u>Insurance</u>: There are many types of insurance policies that parties to a reality television agreement require, including the following: entertainment package policies, comprehensive general liability, errors and omissions, worker's compensation, automobile liability, employer liability, and cast insurance. Each reality television contract requires different insurance coverage. For example, an on-air talent agreement will address cast insurance, and a production services agreement will most likely require all of the above insurance coverages. Entertainment package policies not only cover cast and crew insurance, but also will address issues relevant to each reality show including negative film and videotape insurance, faulty stock, camera and processing insurance, adverse weather, extra expense and rain insurance, props, sets, and wardrobe insurance in addition to other comprehensive and property liability insurance. Some of the issues attorneys address are the individuals and companies that are covered by such insurance, whether or not specific insurance is required to be obtained, which party is required to obtain it, the minimum amount of coverage, the maximum amount of deductible, how long such insurance coverage is required to be in force, whether any exclusion from coverage are allowed, and the terms concerning any physical exams that are required to cover any individual. If an individual has any health or other physical problems, the attorneys will also negotiate the terms regarding the effect of any such health or other problems and the consequences if they make an individual uninsurable.

10) <u>Non-Guild Agreement</u>: The exact numbers are not known, but there are very few reality television productions that are signatory to any guild or union. It is much less expensive to produce reality shows without paying the minimum salary amounts, in addition to pension, health, residual, and other amounts that are required by producers and production companies that are signatories to a guild or union. Most reality television contracts contain terms that require the show and all services provided be provided by individuals who are not members of any guild or union. There have been some strikes by writers, editors, and crew working on high-profile reality television shows that have resulted in a contentious outcome: the termination of the striking workers or, in the alternative, in a more amicable manner; that is, a settlement where a show agreed to become a guild signatory. This process has been on a show-by-show basis and the facts of each specific situation—that is, union or non-union—is reflected in this paragraph of each contract for such shows. Some of the more widely known reality shows that have had striking workers include *The Biggest Loser, Shahs of Sunset, Fashion Police, America's Next Top Model*, and *Survivor*.

11) <u>Applicable Law/Venue</u>: The laws of a particular state will govern the interpretation of the agreement and the resolution of any disputes between the parties. It is customary that the party that has the most leverage in any negotiation will be able to choose which state's laws will be applicable. However, the parties' attorneys will negotiate and request a particular state's laws if it is advisable based on the specific situation of their client or reality show. The venue is the place where any dispute would occur. It is customary that the parties will be required to be present at the proceeding adjudicating any dispute, so the locations of the parties are a consideration in the negotiations.

12) <u>Arbitration</u>: Most all reality television contracts include a provision that the parties agree to bring any dispute to arbitration. There are many terms that are included in the arbitration paragraph, including the organization that the parties agree will bring their arbitration to

adjudicate their dispute. The American Arbitration Association (AAA) and JAMS (formerly known as Judicial Arbitration and Mediation Services) are two common organizations chosen. In general, filing and defending an arbitration claim is expensive when compared to filing a lawsuit because the parties are required to pay the arbitration organization fee, rental of a room at the arbitration organization, the daily fee of the arbitrator or arbitrators, and other costs. The parties will include in this paragraph what costs are required to be incurred and which party is required to pay such costs. There are other basic rights that parties have when filing a lawsuit—for example, the right to demand the other party to provide documents and other evidence to assist settling the dispute—that are not automatically available to the parties in an arbitration. The parties' attorneys will also want to discuss including such rights in this paragraph so that it is clear that the parties agreed to have such rights should they go to arbitration. It is standard that arbitration is agreed to be "binding," which means that the parties are required to accept the arbitration decision with no appeal to a third party to review the decision except in narrow circumstances such as fraud. For certain reality television individuals, such as participants in a reality show, the terms of clauses such as "arbitration" are not negotiable, leaving the participant in a "take it or leave it" position.

PART II:

Development

3

Talent Attachment Agreement

"UNTITLED REALITY SHOW" ON-CAMERA TALENT ATTACHMENT AGREEMENT

Producers often create an idea for a reality show based on a specific person (*Keeping Up With the Kardashians*), a type of person (The *Real Housewives* franchise), or a business (*Rob Dyrdek's Fantasy Factory*). Producers may also base an unscripted show on the ideas and/or existing intellectual property of another (*Rich Kids of Instagram*).

Once the producer has settled on a concept, the producer must seek out the services of on-camera talent that can carry an entire show and who will resonate with viewers. An eye for talent can make the difference between being a person with great ideas and being a producer with television shows on the air. In scripted television, producers rely on professional writers and actors. In contrast, the on-camera talent featured in unscripted television programs plays a significant role in guiding the direction of the show and is is responsible for drawing in an audience. If the program is a docu-series, the story and the day-to-day life of the on-camera talent will guide the direction of the program. If the program requires a host or an expert in a particular field, it is important that the person be both knowledgeable and credible.

Once the producer decides on the on-camera talent for a particular concept, the producer presents the talent with an attachment agreement. In today's programming landscape, there are more reality television producers and networks interested in airing unscripted programming than ever, and the competition for on-camera talent can be fierce. By the time a producer discovers a fascinating family, business, online persona, etc. it is likely that other producers have already approached the potential talent with similar interest. This "attachment agreement" gives the producer the exclusive right to present the on-camera talent and the project to potential buyers for a limited period of time. If the talent is essential to the project or the talent's on-camera participation will help sell the project, the producer must enter into an agreement with the talent before pitching the show.

The most savvy on-camera talent, even those with no on-camera experience, will hire an entertainment lawyer who specializes in unscripted television to help negotiate his or her attachment agreement. A talent agreement can attach the talent to the producer for years, and getting out of a legally binding agreement is never as easy as entering into one. Moreover, if the proposed television show features the on-camera talent's intellectual property or business, the stakes are often much greater. Many networks now require a percentage share of any business revenue that is attributable to the on-camera talent's participation on the show. It is imperative that the on-camera talent understands the potential long-term effects of signing an agreement.

Once the on-camera talent signs the agreement, the producer can begin "shopping" the project (i.e., the producer can develop and submit the project to potential television networks with the on-camera talent "attached"). Upon set-up (i.e., the producer receives a commitment from a buyer to purchase or fund the development and/or production of the project) the on-camera talent will continue to be "attached" if the network and producer decide to engage the talent's services (i.e., the talent is committed to providing on-camera services for a pilot/ presentation and/or the initial series of episodes).

The following is a typical attachment agreement (also known as a shopping agreement) between the producer and the on–camera talent.

RE: "Untitled Reality Project"

Dear [Artist Name]:

This confirms the agreement ("Agreement") between you, _____ ("Artist"), and _____ ("Producer"), for the purpose of developing, producing, and exploiting a television series, special, or series of specials based upon _____ (the "Project"). The agreed terms are as follows:

> The producer is the person or production company who develops and submits the project to potential buyers (i.e., broadcast networks, cable or satellite networks, studios, financiers, and distributors) to determine the buyers' interest in the project. The producers' objective is to obtain the buyers' commitment to finance, develop, produce, purchase, distribute, and/or exploit the project. The producer does not purchase the rights to the project from the talent or any other party; the producer only promises to solicit the interest of potential buyers and to produce the pilot and/or series (i.e., the production of the program will "run through" the producer) once the project is sold.
>
> The artist is the on-camera talent whom the producer would like featured in the television pilot and/or series if the project is produced. The talent may be a celebrity, an unknown personality who was discovered by the producer, a person who created the concept and features prominently in the proposed project, or an expert in a particular field. Anyone whom the producer believes would make interesting television could be the next reality television star.
>
> The project is the name of the proposed television show (also known as the "working title").
>
> The parties may also elect to define the concept of the project in the introductory paragraph, for example a docu-series following talent on his quest to find love in small-town Iowa. If the concept of the project is not defined, it may be difficult to determine with certainty whether either party is violating the terms of the talent attachment agreement at the expiration of the agreement (see section 12 below).

ATTACHING ARTIST AND ARTIST'S BUSINESS:
If the concept is based on the talent and a business owned by the talent, the agreement will contain additional terms that specifically relate to the producer's attachment of the business to the project.

The introductory paragraph might be amended as follows:

This confirms the agreement ("Agreement") between you, _____ ("Artist"), and _____ ("Producer"), for the purpose of developing, producing, and exploiting a television series, special, or series of specials currently entitled _____ (the "Project") featuring Artist and Artist's business (the "Business"). The agreed terms are as follows:

1. Conditions Precedent: Producer's obligations as set forth herein are conditioned upon receipt by Producer of a copy of this Agreement executed by Artist in a form acceptable to Producer.

Before the producer has the legal obligation to fulfill its responsibilities under the agreement, the talent may be required to satisfy certain conditions. The obligations are always specific to the talent, producer, and project. Some examples of common conditions precedent in a talent agreement include:

(1) Receipt by producer of a copy of the agreement signed by each person comprising the on-camera talent (e.g., if the concept is a docu-series featuring a husband and wife, the producer will have no obligation to either individual until both have signed the agreement).

(2) The producer may make all obligations subject to the talent submitting to a customary background check. This may apply if the show features doctors and/or medicine, if the talent is required to drive or operate heavy machinery, or in any other situation where the producer could reasonably foresee a buyer requiring it.

(3) If the project features a musician and will feature music composed and/or performed by the talent, the agreement may be conditioned on the producer's receipt of a signed agreement between the producer and the talent's music publisher granting a master and synchronization license to use the talent's music in connection with the project.

(4)   If there was a prior agreement between the talent and another producer with respect to the project, the current producer may condition its obligation upon receipt and approval of clear chain-of-title for the project. This is especially important if the prior agreement exposes the producer to potential liability (e.g., a per-episode royalty to the former producer or an obligation to accord credit to the prior producer) or prevents the talent from granting certain rights to the project.

2. Talent Hold/Option: In consideration for Producer's efforts to create, develop, and pitch the Project with Artist attached thereto as on-camera talent, for a period of one (1) year following Artist's execution of this Agreement (the "Option Period"), Producer shall have an exclusive option ("Option") to engage Artist as an on-camera performer on and in connection with the Project. During the Option Period, Producer, with Artist's assistance, will approach broadcasting networks (or parents, subsidiaries, or affiliates thereof), or cable or satellite networks (or parents, subsidiaries, or affiliates thereof) (collectively the "Network") to obtain a commitment for purchase or funding for the Project ("Commitment").

The talent hold/option period (or the term of the attachment agreement) is the period of time the producer has to develop and pitch the project to buyers and to obtain a commitment from a buyer to purchase or fund the project. If the talent entered into a shopping agreement or a collaboration agreement with a third party producer (typically, the third party producer discovers the talent but is not rendering production company services on the project) prior to entering into the talent attachment agreement, the option period should mirror the term of the third-party agreement. If the talent agreement is the first agreement that the Producer is entering into in relation to the project, then the length of the talent hold is negotiable. The length of the term can be as short as a few months and as long as a few years.

The talent will want the attachment period to be as short as possible (e.g. 6–9 months), especially if the talent is exclusive to the producer for the option period or if there is heat on the talent (a shorter option period gives a quicker opportunity to get back on the market). This also forces the producer to pitch with urgency and to make this project a priority over other projects the producer is developing and pitching with longer terms. The producer, on the other hand, will want the longest period possible (e.g. 1–2 years). This gives the producer more time to develop the project and to solicit interest from potential buyers. Generally, the parties settle on an attachment term between 9 months and 1 year.

The producer may also request additional time (e.g. 30–90 days) upon the expiration of the term in the form of an automatic extension. If there is an offer from a buyer, the automatic extension provides the buyer the opportunity to continue ongoing negotiations and finalize an agreement. This automatic extension benefits both parties. Otherwise, there would be no incentive for the producer to pitch the project toward the end of the term.

During the attachment period, the producer pitches the project to buyers in an attempt to gauge interest in the project and the on-camera talent with the hopes of getting the project "set up." The talent will be expected to assist producer's efforts in obtaining a commitment for purchase or funding of the project. These services may include attending creative meetings and conferences regarding production matters, attending pitch meetings with potential buyers and/or other financiers, or any other activity that will assist producer's effort to "set up" the project. Other development activities may include access to the talent's day-to-day activities during the development period for the purposes of filming a sizzle reel and assisting the producer in finding additional cast members.

If the talent brought the concept to the producer, the talent might also request that he or she be invited to attend all of the pitch meetings with potential buyers arranged by the producer. If the producer does agree to invite the talent to the pitch meetings, the producer should clarify that the talent will only be invited to in-person pitch meetings and the talent is responsible for bearing all costs associated with attending the meeting (e.g., costs associated with travel, hair, makeup, wardrobe, etc.)

It is important to note that the producer has an option to engage the talent's on-camera services; however, the producer does not have an obligation to do so. If the producer pitches the show to a buyer who wants to purchase the concept but would like to feature on-camera talent of their choosing, the producer is free to sell the show and hire whomever they choose. If the show is a docu-series that follows the life of a specific person or the person is a well-known celebrity, it is unlikely that the project would be sold without the talent's attachment. Conversely, if the show is about a type of person (e.g. *The Real Housewives of Orange County*), the talent is attached as an on-camera host, etc., there is no guarantee that the network and the producer will exercise the option on the talent, even if the project is "set up." Talent representatives will often ask for a guarantee that the talent be attached to the project as the on-camera talent for all episodes produced of the project, but the producer should never agree to this term as it is not something that he or she can absolutely guarantee.

3. Services:
If a Commitment is obtained, then upon Producer's exercise of the Option Artist shall be engaged to render on-camera talent services for a pilot and/or initial series of episodes based on the Project.

Once the program is sold and the buyer elects to engage the talent, the producer will exercise the talent's option and the talent will be committed to rendering on-camera services and any other services that the producer and/or buyer require. In most instances, the talent attachment agreement will only state that the talent will render services customarily rendered by principal talent in connection with unscripted programs. The parties may negotiate and list the services that the talent will render upon "set up" in the talent attachment agreement if there is a specific service the talent refuses to render or if the terms of talent's exclusivity somehow affect the talent's ability to render such services. Once the project is "set up," the network will define the services required of the talent.

ATTACHING ARTIST AND ARTIST'S BUSINESS:
If attaching the talent's business, the talent will also be required to permit access to the business for the purpose of filming day-to-day activities. The producer will also request the talent's assistance in obtaining permission to film on and around the premises of the business, and assistance in procuring clearances to film other individuals affiliated with the business (e.g., employees, clients, etc.). For instance, if the project features the talent and the talent's wedding planning business, the producer will need permission to film at the wedding planner's office, to film at any vendor locations that the wedding planners visit (e.g., bakeries, flower shops, etc.) and to film at the wedding venue. The producer will also need on-camera releases from the talent's staff and from anyone else who appears on camera (e.g., wedding guests, vendors, vendor employees, etc.). Clients of a particular business or companies that the business frequently works with may not be inclined to be featured in the project; therefore, it is important to have a "good faith" or

"best efforts" assurance from the talent that he or she will assist in obtaining permission from their clients. Depending on the producer's vision for the project, there may not be a viable television series without these permissions and clearances in place.

4. Series Options: Provided Artist renders services on an initial season of the Project, Producer shall have five (5) additional, separate, exclusive, consecutive, irrevocable, dependent options (each a "Subsequent Series Option") to engage Artist to render on-camera services, under the same terms and conditions contained herein, for additional seasons of the Project. Subsequent Series Options shall be exercised by Producer in writing, if at all, no later than thirty (30) days following a firm, non-contingent Network order for an additional season of the Project. For purposes hereof, "season" shall be defined as per Producer's agreement with the Network.

If the buyer that purchases the project elects to utilize the talent's on-camera services on the project and the talent's option is exercised, the network will also require additional options to engage the talent's services on the pilot/presentation and on the series. If the project is in its infancy, the producer may not list the options in the attachment agreement. If the producers do not define the options, the language in the talent attachment agreement should reflect that the term will be automatically extended as required by the buyer upon "set up" of the project. If there is already interest in the talent and the project, however, the parties are more likely to agree to subsequent series options whereby the producer will secure exclusive options (usually 4–6) to engage the talent on the project for multiple cycles. If the talent is a celebrity or has some leverage in the negotiations, the number of options may also be negotiated up front, because the talent will want the least number of options possible. The talent may also ask for shorter notice periods, so that they are not held off the market for months at a time while the buyer decides to pick up the show.

The talent's representative will likely request that the talent be guaranteed to appear in a minimum number of episodes per cycle or that the talent will be guaranteed payment for "all shows produced" (i.e., the talent will receive his or her episodic fee for each episode produced in the applicable cycle regardless of whether he or she appears in every episode). The producer should not agree to this at the attachment stage unless the talent is a celebrity or has significant negotiating power, as this has the potential to affect the creative direction of the project and may require payment to the on-camera talent regardless of services actually rendered.

5. Compensation: For any development steps of the Project (i.e., any elements other than a full pilot [airable or non-airable] or a series episode), no fee shall be payable to Artist in connection therewith, unless Producer obtains a fee for any such element(s).

A talent attachment agreement is the most cost-effective approach for a producer to lock key talent to a concept before pitching it to potential buyers. Unless there is heat on the talent (i.e., there is more than one producer interested in creating an unscripted television series based on the talent or a concept created by the talent) or the talent is an established or noteworthy celebrity, the talent attaches his- or herself to the project for free. When the talent's attachment is free to the producer, a legally enforceable contract can only be created if both sides give something else of value (e.g., an agreement to render services or a promise to take action or to refrain from taking action). In the case of a talent attachment agreement where no money is exchanged, the talent grants the free attachment in exchange for the producer's efforts to "set up" the project with the talent attached as on-camera talent. In exchange, the talent makes an agreement to assist in the producer's efforts to set up the project and may make a further promise to hold himself or herself off of the market during the talent attachment period.

In the rare instance that the producer provides an attachment fee to the talent, it can range from several hundred to several thousand dollars depending on the project's nature, significance, and heat on the talent. If the producer does agree to an attachment fee, it should be on a "non-citable non-precedential" basis so that it cannot be used as a negotiating tool against the producer in the future. Alternatively, the producer may agree that no fee will be payable to the talent in connection with any development steps (i.e., any elements other than a full pilot [airable or non-airable] or a series episode) unless the producer receives a fee. Most networks, however, will not agree to pay the on-camera talent a separate fee for his or her development services, and if so the fee is very low (i.e. $250–$1,000). If the network agrees to a development fee for the producer, but not for the talent, then the talent's fee will come from the money paid to the producer for development services.

Of note, because it is difficult to gauge the appropriate fee for the on-camera talent until the project is set up and the buyer agrees to the budget, the talent's episodic fee is almost always negotiated directly with the buyer when the project is "set up" and the talent's option is exercised. Even if the talent has precedent (also known as quotes), it may not be appropriate based on the budget of the show once it is sold. The parties may, however, agree on the compensation in this agreement. This is further discussed in relation to paragraph 7 below.

ATTACHING ARTIST AND ARTIST'S BUSINESS:

The talent will never receive a fee (or additional fee) for attaching his or her business. When the project is sold, however, the talent will either receive an increased on-camera fee or a separate fee as consideration for access to the premises of the business and access to the intellectual property associated with the business.

The talent should also be prepared for the distinct possibility that the television network will claim a stake in any business owned by the talent that is featured on the program. Before *The Real Housewives of New York*, Bethenny Frankel was a relatively unknown chef. After starring on the show, which frequently mentioned Bethenny's Skinnygirl product line, her flagship product, the Skinnygirl Margarita, reportedly sold to Fortune Brands' Beam Global for $100 million. Even though Bravo featured Skinnygirl season after season, the network was not entitled to a single penny from the $100 million sale. As unscripted television has become more and more profitable, most networks now have a policy of retaining a percentage of any revenue attributable to the business being featured on the program. Known in the industry as the "schmuck insurance" provision, the television networks will never miss out on a percentage of a sale of this magnitude again.

ATTACHING ARTIST AND ARTIST'S FAMILY (OR A GROUP ASSOCIATED WITH ARTIST):

If the show features the talent and the talent's family, the producer may acknowledge in the talent attachment agreement that the fee that the talent's family members will be paid will be negotiated in good faith when the project is set up. In the alternative, if the parties negotiate the talent's fee in the attachment agreement, they may raise the fee to include the talent's family members. For instance, if the parties would otherwise agree that the talent would be paid $2,000 per episode; the producer may acknowledge a $5,000 per episode fee, with the additional $3,000 to be split among the talent's family members at the talent's discretion. The same applies if the producer is interested in a group of people associated with the talent (i.e., employees, team-mates, etc.).

6. Exclusivity: During the Option Period (including any extension thereof) and for all periods during which Producer has an unexpired Subsequent Series Option hereunder (collectively, the "Term"), Artist shall be exclusive to Producer as (an) or (the) on-camera performer in series television throughout the universe.

The level of exclusivity to the producer during the attachment period is also negotiable, and may be as restrictive as prohibiting the talent from rendering on-camera services in any form of media and as permissive as only requiring the talent to be available for development activities and pitching.

Depending on the prior experience of the talent, the current projects and agreements for which talent is currently engaged, and the type of media for which the project is intended (i.e., web, network television, subscription video on demand [Netflix], etc.) the talent may negotiate carve-outs for specific projects or negotiate for looser exclusivity provisions. Some exclusivity examples that may be used in the talent attachment agreement include:

(i) Artist shall be exclusive to Producer, and Artist shall not provide any services whatsoever for any other producer.

(ii) Artist shall be exclusive in all forms of reality/unscripted television programming in all media (including any reality/unscripted programming produced for the internet); provided Artist shall be permitted to render services in connection with scripted television and theatrical motion pictures.

(iii) Artist shall be exclusive in all reality/unscripted television programming and all programming with a format or concept similar to the project in all media.

(iv) Artist shall be permitted to render services in connection with Artist's standup comedy engagements.

(v)   Artist shall be permitted to render services in connection with internet programs featuring Artist, so long as the internet programs are not similar to the Project (i.e., not a docu-series style program).

(vi) Artist shall be permitted to participate as a host or judge in connection with reality/unscripted television programming.

If the producer does not require complete exclusivity, the producer should require that none of the services permitted will materially interfere with the talent's services for the producer. The producer should also request that the project be in first position (i.e., the project is the first priority over all other projects).

The talent may also request that certain projects are "carved out." A "carve-out" is when something is excluded from a particular obligation in an agreement. An "exclusivity carve-out" is used when the parties agree to a certain level of exclusivity, but the talent is permitted to render some services that would otherwise violate the exclusivity clause in the agreement. The talent may request a carve-out permitting him or her to continue rendering services relating to projects that pre-date the talent attachment agreement. For example, if a company wanted to shop a daytime talk show featuring Padma Lakshmi, they would have to carve out her continued services on *Top Chef*, as this is an agreement that pre-dates her talk show. If the talent does not make the producer aware of his or her pre-existing contractual obligations, continuing services on the other project may violate the exclusivity requirements of the talent agreement, which would put the talent in breach. Another type of carve-out that the talent might ask for permits the talent to continue rendering a certain type of service that would otherwise violate the agreement. For example, if the talent is prohibited from rendering services for another reality television project (which generally includes docu-series, reality competitions, game shows, talk shows, variety shows, news, and news magazine programming), the talent may request that one or more reality categories be carved out. If the project is a docu-series, but the talent makes regular appearances as an expert on news shows, the parties may agree that the talent is exclusive in all reality television but can make any number of appearances on news programming, so long as the docu-series remains the first priority. This carve-out is generally reserved for talent who are already involved in the type of programming that is excluded (i.e., a desire to parlay the project into television news appearances is not enough).

Unless the talent is a celebrity, there is a lot of interest from potential buyers, or the carve-out is reasonable, the network will not usually permit the on-camera talent to render any services whatsoever for any other program. This includes scripted or unscripted programming intended for broadcast on any other network, cable, or digital/online television outlets. Even though it will be difficult to negotiate for anything other than absolute exclusivity, the parameters and arguments used for the talent attachment agreement are the same arguments that can be used to negotiate with the buyer once the project is "set up."

ATTACHING ARTIST AND ARTIST'S BUSINESS:
If attaching a business, the business must be exclusive to the producer, and at the very least exclusive with respect to all types of similar/competitive programming. A television network would never agree to purchase a project following a particular business if another project featuring the same business is also being developed. With this in mind, the producer should make every effort to obtain 100% exclusivity over the talent's business in all media in all territories.

7. Production of the Program: If Producer obtains the Commitment and exercises the Option, the terms and conditions regarding Artist's Services, including the fee that will be paid to Artist, Artist's exclusivity, and credit accorded to Artist, shall be set forth in a separate agreement to be negotiated by Producer with Network on Artist's behalf in good faith in accordance with industry and Producer's standards for similar shows (with due regard for the budget and license fee of the show), for similar services for persons of similar stature and experience.

If the producer obtains a commitment from a buyer (and the buyer exercises its option to engage the talent to render on-camera services), the terms and conditions of the talent's services for the project, including the talent's fee, credit, and exclusivity, are negotiated by the talent directly with the buyer (or with the producer if the buyer requires) in a separate agreement. The talent attachment agreement will generally state that such negotiation will be done in good faith within the budgetary parameters of the project.

If the talent owns the intellectual property the show is based on, is a celebrity, or has leverage of some kind, the talent may ask to negotiate his or her fee, credit, and exclusivity at the attachment stage. Alternatively, if the producer is concerned that the talent will ask for more than what is appropriate in comparison to persons of similar stature and experience once the project is "set up," the producer may also want to finalize these points during this initial negotiation stage.

Artist's Fee: The fee to the talent may be a flat fee for each episode in which he or she appears or may be a percentage of the budget. The flat fee may be as low as $1,000 per pilot or series episode and can increase significantly depending on what the talent brings to the project (e.g., an idea or a celebrity with a fan base of built in viewers). The fee usually increases by 4–5% for each additional cycle, subject to the buyer's exercise of the applicable cycle option. Alternatively, the fee may be a percentage of the approved budget for each episode (generally, 1–3%). The talent may further require a floor and ceiling to the budget percentage (for example, 1.5% of the buyer-approved budget for each episode, provided that such fee is no less than $10,000 per episode [the floor] and no greater than $15,000 per episode [the ceiling]).

A savvy talent representative will also try to ensure that the talent receives a fee for "all episodes produced" by the producer and will request a minimum guarantee of episodes per cycle. The producer, on the other hand, will only want to pay if the talent appears in the episode and will be hesitant to guarantee that the talent will be featured in or paid for each and every episode of the program.

In addition to the episodic fee, the talent may also request a percentage of the producer's contingent compensation. These proceeds are generally based on a percentage of receipts derived from the exploitation of the series and are paid to the producer by the buyer and/or broadcaster of the series. Because the contingent compensation will be paid directly from the producer's share of the back end, the producer should only grant this when absolutely necessary.

Artist's Exclusivity: Once the project is "set up," any additional exclusivity required by the buyer will be negotiated directly with the buyer as each buyer will have its own exclusivity requirements.

Artist's Credit: For the most part, unscripted agreements are not governed by the Screen Actors Guild-American Federation and Radio Artists ("SAG-AFTRA"); therefore, the talent is not guaranteed credit regardless of the services he or she renders. To protect their clients, talent representatives may request a confirmation that their client will receive a credit, and the terms of such credit. The producer will usually agree to on-screen credit on each episode of the program for which the talent actually appears. Depending on the degree to which the project requires the specific talent's attachment to the project, the producer may also agree to credit on a single card, a credit "tie" to other on-camera performers (i.e. the talent's credit will be a similar size and style as all others rendering similar services), and even a producer or origination credit, depending on the talent's role in creating the concept the project is based on and the additional services the talent intends to render during production. Notwithstanding these credit "guarantees," the producer will make any credit offer in the attachment agreement subject to the approval of the applicable buyer. This protects the producer from agreeing to a term that might encumber the sale of the project if the buyer does not want to agree to the credit provisions offered by the producer.

8. Approvals: Artist shall have a meaningful consultation right with Producer on the creative elements of the Project. Additionally, once in production, Artist shall have a meaningful consultation right with Producer on all key creative elements of the Project; however, in the event of a good faith disagreement, Producer's decision shall control.

If the talent is a celebrity, the right to control how his or her image is displayed on-camera will likely be one of the most important deal points in the negotiation. Similarly, if the talent created the idea or intellectual property, they will be hesitant to release their control over the project to a producer. On the other hand, the producer will push back and will not want to give approvals or consultation unless there is a chance the producer will lose the talent, and therefore the project. The standard compromise is to give the talent a "meaningful consultation right." The parties will then negotiate what the consultation or approval right extends to. Some examples of meaningful consultation include:

- Key creative decisions with respect to the theme and format of the program

- The other key talent

- The buyers that producer can pitch and sell the show

- The director of the program

The talent will want any approval or consultation rights to continue after the show is "set up," so that they are meaningfully consulted for the life of the project.

If the producer has to agree to approvals or consultation rights, the producer will want to clarify that if the producer fails to consult with the talent it will not be considered a breach of the agreement, the consultation right will be exercised by talent in a reasonable manner and, most importantly, in the event of a disagreement the producer's decision will control.

9. Non-Union: See Chapter 2

The unions do not govern the vast majority of unscripted television shows. Unlike scripted television programming, where union membership is compulsory, the producer and the network decide whether or not an unscripted television show will be a signatory to the various union agreements. As amateur on-camera performers without guild safeguards, reality-show participants have relatively few legal protections.

Not surprisingly, producers and networks are reluctant to become signatories to the SAG-AFTRA agreement when refusing to do so keeps the budgets low (with no minimum guaranteed payment per episode) thereby keeping profits high. Although some reality shows are covered by SAG-AFTRA (the guild that represents on-camera talent), including network hits such as *Survivor, Amazing Race, Dancing with the Stars, American Idol, Jeopardy,* and *Judge Judy,* becoming a SAG-AFTRA signatory generally only occurs when there are real and tangible benefits to the producer and the network (for example, the ability to hire SAG-AFTRA hosts and celebrity talent).

The unions initially ignored unscripted television; however, now that these television shows generate big audiences and big business, the unions are looking to change their role in the unscripted space. Unscripted producers, talent, and their representatives would be wise to follow the evolution of the union's role in unscripted television, as the status quo is unlikely to last much longer.

10. Results and Proceeds/Grant of Rights/Rights: See Chapter 2

ATTACHING ARTIST AND ARTIST'S BUSINESS:
When negotiating for the attachment of the talent's business, the results and proceeds will differ in one significant way: the talent must clarify that he or she will retain the business's pre-existing intellectual property (e.g. logos, trademarks, etc.) and other property relating to the business. The producer should not have an interest in the talent's business aside from the project and the exploitation of the project. The producer will not take issue with this; however, the talent's representative should remind the talent that although the producer will not require an interest in the talent's business, upon "set up" the network may require a royalty based on the success of the talent's business after the show airs.

11. Name/Likeness/Biography: If Producer obtains the Commitment and exercises the Option, Artist hereby grants to Producer the perpetual, non-exclusive right, but not the obligation, to use and authorize others to use Artist's name(s), voice, image, photograph, personal characteristics, actual or simulated likeness, expressions, performance, attributes, personal experiences, and biographical information (collectively "Name and Likeness") in and in connection with the production, distribution, advertising, publicity, promotion, merchandising, exhibition, and other exploitation of all versions and formats of the Project (including its title) and the businesses and/or programs of Network, Producer, and their licensees, sublicensees, and assigns (including all advertising, publicity and promotion, and materials associated therewith) and in or in connection with any episode of the Project in which Artist does not appear, including without limitation in billing, cast credits, advertising, promoting or publicizing any such episode, in any manner, in any and all media and by any means now known or hereafter devised (including, but not limited to, use in and in connection with publishing, tie-ins, and merchandise, as well as in connection with or on materials which package or enclose any such items). No additional payment shall be required for any such uses, unless otherwise specified in this Agreement. Producer may include photographs or other images or depictions of the likeness of Artist in or in relation to any exploitation of the Project and all documentaries, "behind-the-scenes," "the making of" featurettes, promotional films, and videos of the Project in any manner and by any means throughout the universe, subject to Artist's prior, written approval, such approval not to be unreasonably withheld.

Approvals: The talent's representative will almost always request that the talent be given approval over the use of the talent's name, likeness, and biography. This request, however, will only be granted if the talent is established in the industry or has precedent (i.e., prior deals in which the talent was granted this right) and if the talent is the primary talent on the project. The producer will want the unfettered ability to use the talent's name and likeness (in connection with the program featuring talent *and* any other program that may want to use the footage), and the network will often require it. It can be burdensome for the network's public relations group to get approval over every image, and the details and format of a biography submitted by the talent may not fit the intended use. The talent representative may also request approval over the talent's name and likeness in connection with all documentaries, "behind-the-scenes," "making of" featurettes, promotional films, and videos of the project. As with name, likeness, and biography approval, it is even more unlikely that a network will agree to this for unscripted talent. If it is agreed to, the talent will most certainly be a high-level celebrity.

The network will only agree to this for a celebrity because the celebrity has a brand to protect; even someone with leverage in an agreement (i.e., multiple offers from other producers) does not likely have the brand recognition to warrant such a protection. If the producer absolutely must agree, it is important that the producer include language stating that the talent's approval over any image, biography, or footage featuring the talent will not be unreasonably withheld or delayed. Otherwise, the talent would not be obligated to approve any materials.

Use in advertising, publicity, commercial tie-ins, and merchandising: The talent's representative might also ask for a merchandising royalty for the use of the talent's name and likeness on merchandising and other promotional commercial products (5% is the standard, reducible to 2.5% if other individuals who are entitled to a royalty for use of their likeness are also included in the merchandise). The producer should only agree to this if the talent does not get a percentage of the contingent compensation received by the producer and if the talent is a celebrity or has some leverage. The network will usually take the stance that any per-episode or per-season fee paid to the talent includes the right to use talent's name and likeness in connection with advertising, publicity, commercial tie-ins, and merchandising for the show. Where appropriate, however, the network will grant the 5% merchandising royalty. At the talent attachment stage, the producer must make a judgment call as to whether or not a network is likely to agree. The producer should only agree to merchandising royalty for the talent if, in its view, the network is likely to agree.

12. Project Ownership: Artist acknowledges and agrees that, as between Producer and Artist, Producer is the exclusive owner, in perpetuity and throughout the universe, of all right, title, and interest in and to the Project, including the title, concept, themes, format, characters, stories, and all other contents thereof, and all translations, adaptations, sequels, and other versions thereof, and in and to the copyright thereof and all renewals and extensions of such copyright, including without limitation the exclusive right to produce and distribute in all media now known or hereafter devised all types of audiovisual works of any kind based upon the Project and allied rights therein (including by way of illustration all soundtrack, music publishing, and merchandising rights).

If the project is not "set up" with a buyer, the talent attachment agreement should address who owns the project and who owns the development materials created during the attachment period.

If the producer creates the concept, upon the expiration of the term, the producer will generally not have any further obligation to the talent in connection with the project, and the producer will remain the sole and exclusive owner of the idea and any materials created during the attachment period. When the term expires, the producer can pitch the show with other on-camera talent attached without obligation to the original talent.

If the talent creates the concept and the project is not "set up," then the fairest resolution is to allow the talent to proceed without any additional obligations to the producer. However, the producer will want to limit the right so that it does not include a reversion or other transfer to the talent of any right in or to any materials developed by or on behalf of the producer during the attachment period. The producer may provide talent the option to purchase the material (e.g., the cost of creating the materials plus interest) if the talent wants to continue with the project without the producer's involvement. Further, the producer will want to remain attached to the project for a short period following the expiration of the attachment period if the talent sets-up the project with a buyer (this is known as the tail or the protection period). A good rule of thumb is to keep the "tail" the same length as the attachment period—for example, if the term of the talent's attachment to the project is six months, then the "tail" that keeps producer attached to the project should also be six months. The talent will often request an automatic reversion of the development materials without payment to the producer and will try to get rid of a tail completely.

If the talent and producer create the concept together, then any combination of the above may apply. This, as with everything else in the talent attachment agreement, is a negotiation point between the parties. One example of how this might be negotiated provides that all rights in and to the concept and the project will revert to the talent;

provided, however: (a) producer shall have a lien on the concept and the project in an amount equal to the actual out-of-pocket monies expended by producer in connection with the setup and/or development of the program during the attachment period; and (b) in the event talent enters into an agreement with a buyer in connection with production of the Program within 12 months following the expiration of the term, and producer does not also enter into such agreement, producer will receive a royalty in an amount equal to $2,500 for each episode of the Program produced and 5% of 100% of all contingent compensation payable to talent in connection with the project.

13. Representations and Warranties: See Chapter 2

ATTACHING ARTIST AND ARTIST'S BUSINESS:

When attaching a business, the producer may want to consider adding additional representations and warranties to the talent attachment agreement so that there are no surprises when the producer "sets up" the project with a buyer. Most importantly, the producer should ask the talent to represent and warrant that the talent has the right to enter into the agreement, that the talent has the sole authority to grant the producer all of the rights set forth in the agreement, and that the talent and the business will perform all of the obligations set forth in the agreement. The producer should further clarify that any and all creative contributions to the program made by the "business" or the talent's employees are original with the talent and will neither infringe or violate the rights of any third party (including rights of privacy), nor be defamatory. Above all else, the producer needs a commitment from the talent that there are no other rights or commitments in favor of a third party that could impair, interfere with, or infringe upon the rights being granted in the talent attachment agreement, and that the talent, on behalf of the business, has obtained or will obtain all required permission or grants of authority that may be necessary with respect to fulfilling the obligations required in the talent agreement.

14. Indemnification: See Chapter 2

15. Assignment: See Chapter 2

16. No Obligation: See Chapter 2

17. Injunctive Relief: See Chapter 2

18. Applicable Law: See Chapter 2

19. Miscellaneous: The Parties agree that all provisions and/or terms not discussed herein, which are normally included in similar instruments (e.g., force majeure, limitation of remedies, termination, and suspension) shall be subject to good faith negotiations within customary industry parameters for productions of the type to be produced hereunder.

20. Binding Agreement: Unless and until the Parties enter into a more detailed, formal agreement, this Agreement shall constitute a binding agreement between the Parties, shall supersede any prior or contemporaneous agreements, and may not be waived or amended, except by a written instrument signed by both Parties. This Agreement may be executed in one or more separate counterparts, each of which, when executed, shall be deemed to be an original. Such counterparts shall, together, constitute and be one and the same agreement.

Very truly yours,

_____

ACCEPTED AND AGREED:

Producer   **Artist**

_____   By: _____

NAME, President   **NAME**

DEAL POINT CHECKLIST
Talent Attachment Agreement

1. Satisfaction of Conditions Precedent
2. Talent Hold / Option Exercise Date
3. Artist's Services / Producer's Expectations
4. Exclusivity during the Attachment Period
5. Series Pick-Up and Series Options
   - Series Exercise Date
   - Number of Subsequent Options
   - Episodic Fee and Per Cycle Increases to the Artist's Episodic Fee
   - Episodic Guarantee
   - Exclusivity required by the Network
   - Credit
6. Consultation Rights
7. Name, Likeness, and Biography Approval
8. Merchandising
   - Approval over Merchandising Use
   - Royalty for Merchandising Use
9. Project Ownership

REPRESENTING PRODUCTION COMPANIES: TELEVISION PACKAGES

Representation by a reputable talent agency is essential to an unscripted production company's success. The talent agent helps the production company strategize the best way to sell a particular show, introduces the production company to potential buyers, and can direct the production company toward a particular type of show that a network is looking for. While everyone thinks they have the next great reality television show idea, the talent agency serves as a gatekeeper for potential buyers. It can be difficult, if not impossible, to get in a room with a network executive without the support of a talent agent. Association with a talent agent tells the buyer that the idea has been vetted and the production company can be trusted with hundreds of thousands of dollars to turn a pitch into a successful television series. The agent may also introduce the production company to showrunners, on-camera talent, or other producers that will help develop and sell the show. To generate the best deal possible, the agent will also work to create "heat" and excitement around the project, which can lead to a bidding war, driving up the price and the options available to the production company.

For its services, a talent agency usually receives a commission, typically 10% of the client's gross earnings, including but not limited to contingent compensation, royalties, bonuses, etc. In the case of a production company, the talent agent receives 10% of the client's producer fees or production fee (typically 10% of the budget) and 10% of any other fees payable to the production company for their services. The talent agency may elect to forgo its commission for a "package" participation in a project. An unscripted television package follows the 3-10 model: the agency receives 3% of the total production budget, paid upon delivery of each episode, and 10% of back-end participation derived from the exploitation of the series taken "off the top" (i.e., the back end is paid to the agency before anyone else receives their back-end participation). The agency will further assert that the package applies to any other projects based on or derived from the project (e.g., remakes, sequels, spin-offs, specials, etc.). These packaging fees are built into the cost of producing the show.

Whether the talent agency receives a package (or not) is based on leverage—does the agency have an element that the buyer needs (i.e. star talent, the show creator, etc.). In the case of a producer or a production company who creates and develops a television program, the answer to that question is always yes. If a buyer refuses to grant a package to an agency, the agency may decide to simply take the project elsewhere. If the talent agency receives a "package" on a project (which will be contractually recognized in the Production Services Agreement), the buyer pays the agency (e.g., a television network, studio, or other buyer) and the talent does not owe additional commission to the talent agency.

In 2014, the website The Wrap[1] revealed that non-scripted TV packaging had generated $61 million for William Morris Endeavor. The budget for an unscripted television show can range from $100,000 to more than $500,000 per episode (and usually escalates season to season), resulting in thousands of dollars paid to the talent agency for each episode produced. Even if the client leaves the series or the talent agency, the agency retains the package. A package can be highly lucrative for a talent agency on a successful series. Once a series is sold into syndication, the talent agency stands to gain millions from its back-end participation. For example, William Morris has made $16 million from packaging fees from its back-end participation in connection with *Who Wants to Be a Millionaire*.

---

1   www.thewrap.com/leaked-inside-details-of-two-billion-dollar-wme-img-financing/

4

Collaboration Agreement Between Two Production Companies

"UNTITLED REALITY SHOW" AGREEMENT BETWEEN PRODUCTION COMPANIES TO COLLABORATE ON AN UNSCRIPTED TELEVISION SHOW

A collaboration agreement for unscripted television is a contract between two people or companies, in this case producers or production companies, who agree to develop an unscripted television idea in order to sell it to a potential financier or network for production. In this agreement, the parties will define rights and obligations of the parties, including but not limited to the length of the agreement, how the responsibilities will be allocated, who controls creative and business decisions, how profits will be divided, who owns the idea if the project does not sell, and any other terms that may be applicable to the specific project or the parties.

A collaboration agreement should be negotiated and signed before either party pitches the project. It would be foolish to enter into a business venture without drafting an agreement between the parties. Show creators must treat their relationship with the same mindfulness. Before the parties expend time and effort in developing an idea into a television project, it is best to address and resolve any potential issues. Moreover, having an agreement in place before pitching a project is particularly important, because it informs the negotiations between the parties and a buyer (i.e., a television network) when the project is sold. When successful, the relationship between the parties can last for years. With that in mind, it is imperative that each party disclose their expectations to the other party from the outset. Memorializing these expectations in a collaboration agreement can make all the difference between a long and prosperous relationship and a costly lawsuit to settle the disagreements between the collaborators.

This chapter describes the terms of a collaboration agreement between two production companies who intend to develop, pitch, and exploit an unscripted television program.

Re: "Name of the Reality Show We Are Collaborating On"

Dear _____:

This letter sets forth the terms of the agreement (the "Agreement") between Reality TV Production Company, Inc. ("Company 1") and Second Reality TV Production Company, Inc. ("Company 2") (collectively referred to as the "Parties") for the term set forth in Paragraph 1 below, for the purpose of developing, producing, and exploiting an unscripted show currently entitled "Name of the Reality Show We Are Collaborating On" (the "Project").

Before drafting and negotiating a collaboration agreement, it is important to clarify what each party will contribute to the partnership. This will affect the rights and obligations of each party throughout the collaborative process and will determine how the rights are divided if the idea is not set up with a buyer and/or financier at the expiration of the term. Typically, when two producers (or production companies) come together to collaborate on a project, one producer has an idea or has an agreement with on-camera talent

> ("Company 2") and the other has the experience to transform the idea into a television show and the connections to sell the show to a television network ("Company 1"). Once the collaboration agreement is in place, the two parties work together to continue to develop the idea for the purpose of setting it up with a financier or television network.

For good and valuable consideration, the receipt and adequacy of which is hereby acknowledged, the Parties agree as follows:

1. Term: The term of this Agreement will commence on the Date hereof and shall continue through one (1) year from the date that this Agreement is signed by all of the Parties ("Term"). The Parties agree that at the end of the Term if any development, pilot, special, and/or series based on the Project has not been ordered by a Network (defined below), and then any and all rights regarding the Project will revert in accordance with Paragraph 6. It is understood and agreed by the Parties that if active, bona fide negotiations regarding the Project with a Network are occurring at such time that would otherwise be the end of the Term, and then the Term shall be extended for ninety (90) days to permit the conclusion of such negotiations for the Project.

> The standard length of a collaboration agreement is similar to that of a shopping agreement. Company 2 will want to request a shorter term (i.e., six to nine months) so that Company 1 is compelled to immediately devote significant time and resources to assist in setting up the project. If Company 1 has a large slate of projects that it is developing and pitching with other producers and production companies, a short time period is one way that Company 2 can ensure that its project is a priority. Likewise, if there is no immediate interest in the project as pitched by the parties or if Company 1 is not devoting the attention to the project that Company 2 expected when entering into the agreement, Company 2 will benefit from a quick reversion so that it can redevelop and pitch the idea (perhaps with greater success) without Company 1's attachment.
>
> Company 1 will of course want more time to develop and pitch the project. Depending on the type of unscripted project (i.e., docu-series, dating game, talent contest, competition,

game show, etc.) and what Company 2 brought into the collaboration, the parties may need to scout talent, negotiate agreements with the talent, develop the look and feel of the project, shoot a sizzle reel, create a written format and series bible, create potential character and story arcs for the first season, or do any other business or creative planning that may be required to pitch the idea. Company 1 may be able to negotiate for a longer term (i.e., one year or more) depending on the amount of work that needs to be done by the parties.

It should be noted that the traditional arguments relating to the appropriate length of the term for a collaboration agreement are changing to reflect changes in the industry. In the past, the length of the collaboration agreement would reflect the time of year, allowing the companies the opportunity to take full advantage of the traditional development season. Under the traditional model, television shows are pitched from late July through August. Once development season was over, the opportunity to sell a project to a network was almost obsolete. However, the traditional development season is morphing as cable and new media "networks" have started to pick up shows year-round. Unscripted shows are also very attractive mid-season replacements for those following the traditional development season model, as they can be cheap and quick to make.

Another point to be negotiated is whether the term will be extended for an additional period to finalize negotiations with a potential buyer. Concluding the agreement with the buyer is the last step in actually selling the project. Both parties benefit from agreeing to extend the term to conclude negotiations.

Company 1 will want the term to be extended for as long as the parties are in negotiations, arguing that it cannot control the response time of the buyer. Moreover, a finite number of days to negotiate could encourage Company 2 to act in bad faith to drag out the negotiations in hopes of making a deal without Company 1 attached. This would permit Company 2 to effectively circumvent Company 1 by negotiating directly with the buyer at the conclusion of the term without Company 1's attachment.

- The Term shall be extended for ninety (90) days to permit the conclusion of active bona fide (i.e., good faith) negotiations.

- The Term shall be extended day-for-day for a period equal to the duration of ongoing bona fide negotiations.

Company 2's representative should require a cap on the number of days rather than agreeing to an unlimited amount of time to conclude negotiations. This puts the parties and the potential buyer on notice as to the number of days they have to conclude a deal. The parties will usually agree to a 30–90 day extension to accommodate such negotiations.

Examples of languages the companies might agree to include:

The parties may also permit extensions of the term for reasons other than to accommodate ongoing negotiations, e.g. by mutual agreement of the parties, for the duration of any force majeure event (see Chapter 2), or for a period equal to the duration of any agreement entered into by the parties with a buyer for the financing, development, and/ or production of the project.

2. Disposition of the Project: During the Term, the Parties shall have the exclusive right to develop the Project and approach major broad-casting networks (or parents, subsidiaries, or affiliates thereof), or major cable or satellite networks (or parents, subsidiaries, or affiliates thereof) or other buyer or financier (collectively "Network") for development, purchase, or funding for the Project.

Company 1 will want to clarify that the agreement is "exclusive." If the project is "exclusive" to the parties, Company 2 cannot enter into an agreement with another producer or production company to simultaneously develop and pitch the project. Likewise, Company 1 may want to clarify in the collaboration agreement that Company 2 will not have an independent right to shop the idea to third party buyers without Company 1's attachment during the term. In this regard, if Company 2 pitches and sells the project unbeknownst to Company 1 during the term, then Company 1 would still be attached. The agreement will almost always be exclusive, unless it was a material deal point discussed at the outset. Otherwise, there would be no incentive for Company 1 to develop and pitch on the project. Even worse, potential buyers do not want to be pitched the same project twice and would be furious to hear that they were in negotiations with Company 1 and Company 2 only to learn that another producer is also developing the project separately on Company 2's behalf.

The companies may also want to agree to keep each other promptly apprised of all submissions of the project to potential buyers during the term and to keep each other informed of meetings and discussions concerning the project. Company 2 will also want the list of submissions in writing, as they will want a record of whether Company 2 will be attached at the expiration of the term (see paragraph 6 below relating to reversion of rights for more information). If both companies are actively pitching the project, they will of course want to keep each other informed of the other potential submissions so that they do not double submit the project, which could waste valuable time, money, and resources.

(a) If within the Term any development, pilot, special, and/or series based on the Project has been ordered by a Network, then Company 1 shall negotiate the terms and conditions of Company 1's rights and engagements and Company 2 shall negotiate the terms and conditions of Company 2's engagement and rights with the applicable Network, including, without limitation, any fees, contingent compensation, bonuses, services, exclusivity, etc., provided, however, the Parties acknowledge and agree that any such agreement(s) must include and conform to the following terms as a condition precedent to the operation of Paragraph 5 of this Agreement:

The terms that each company will agree to if a third party wants to purchase or sell the project may be set forth in the collaboration agreement. The companies may, on the other hand, elect to leave some or all of the terms up to good faith negotiation with the buyer once the project is actually sold. Whether or not the companies negotiate the terms up front will depend on the level of experience of both of the parties, the type of project, the expected budget of the project, and the buyers who are likely to be the best fit for the project.

Some of the terms that the companies may negotiate up front relate to compensation, credit, the level of services each company will render, and the terms of exclusivity (which are usually determined by the level of services the company and its executives intend to render). If it is a true co-production, and both parties will provide production company services, the deal will likely be 50/50 in terms of compensation, back-end, credit, etc.

If the parties do not agree to any of the aforementioned terms in the collaboration agreement, both companies may want to clarify that the negotiations should be confined to the precedent of each company and the company's executives, and the budgetary parameters of the project. The companies will also likely agree to negotiate so as not to frustrate the timely development and/or production of the project. Even though agreeing to enter into a collaboration agreement implies the sentiment, it should be memorialized in the agreement to protect the companies in the event one company acts in bad faith once there is interest in the project from a third-party buyer.

When the project is sold, both companies will want the opportunity to negotiate on their own behalf directly with the buyer. However, the buyer may want to negotiate directly with the company that pitched the project (i.e. the company that they have a direct relationship with). To address this issue, Company 1 (who likely is bringing industry contacts and experience to the collaboration) may want to clarify that the companies will each negotiate on their own behalf, unless the buyer requires that the terms of Company 2's services be negotiated through Company 1. In this situation, Company 1 helps to facilitate the negotiation so that the buyer only has to negotiate for the rights to the project with one company.

(i)   Mr./Ms. Executive will be an Executive Producer and Co-Creator and will produce the Project through Company 1 which shall also receive applicable credit;

(ii)   Mr./Ms. Executive will be an Executive Producer and Co-Creator and will produce the Project through Company 2 which shall also receive applicable credit;

(iii) Employee of Company ("Employee") will obtain an Executive Producer credit.

The companies will likely negotiate the credit that each company (and the company's executives) will be entitled to in the collaboration agreement rather than wait until the project is sold. The companies may only guarantee credit for the production company; they may negotiate for credits for the company's executives; or both. The specific executive's precedent will likely determine whether a production company executive will receive credit on the project. A buyer is unlikely to agree to a credit for a particular person if that person has no prior credits or experience in the industry.

The credits that the companies usually agree to are: (i) Executive Producer or Co-Producer credit (which is generally dependent on each company's precedent), (ii) origination credit (e.g., "created by" or "concept by"), and (iii) a logo credit (i.e. the production company's logo will appear as an on-screen credit). Networks are particularly sensitive about setting their own precedent when it comes to credits; therefore the buyer may not always agree to the credits agreed to in the collaboration agreement. Company 1 (who has the experience and contacts to likely receive the credit agreed to in the collaboration agreement) will not want to lose a good deal because Company 2's credit requests are not met. Company 1 should always make any agreed-to credit for Company 2 subject to the approval of the applicable network or buyer and, once approved, to the network or buyer policies with respect to such credit.

A savvy negotiator will want to ensure that all production credits are treated equally in all respects (i.e., the credit will be displayed in the same size and style as the other companies' credit) and will further require that their client receive the agreed-to credit on each episode of the program (regardless of services rendered). The companies may further negotiate the order of the cards (i.e., first or second position to the other company's credit), and/or whether such credit is on a single card or if it will be shared with each other or other parties.

Finally, the companies will likely decide at the outset if one company or both will be the production entity for the program. If the production of the program "runs through" one company (likely Company 1), that company generally bears the risk of production overages (i.e., going over budget) and be entitled to retain any so-called production underages (i.e., going under budget).

(b) Net Profits. The Parties agree that concerning any back-end participation and other contingent compensation paid to the Parties in connection with the Project by any third party, or to be otherwise divided between the Parties, that Company 1 will be entitled to fifty percent (50%) and Company 2 will be entitled to fifty percent (50%). The Parties' back-end participation paid by the Network will be defined and accounted for as provided by the Network. The Parties agree that the foregoing split of back-end participation and other contingent compensation for the Project will apply to any and all derivative and subsequent productions of and from the Project and all exploitation of the Project from any source or method now known or hereafter devised.

Collaborators on an unscripted television project usually agree to split all net profits received from the applicable buyer or network on a 50/50 basis. In this situation, the parties pool all of their fees (e.g., company fees, development fees, executive producer fees etc.), bonuses (e.g., pick-up bonuses, ratings bonuses, etc.), and contingent compensation (i.e., profits derived from ancillary rights, merchandising and licensing, distribution rights, derivatives, etc.), and the proceeds from each are split on an equal basis between the parties. The division of proceeds may vary, however, based on the negotiating power and experience of both of the parties. For instance, one company might be a well-established production company while the other company is new to the unscripted world; one company might have to expend a lot more time, resources, and money in order to develop and sell the project; or the project might be "hot" (i.e., there are competing offers on the idea).

The parties may further clarify that if any third-party participants are permitted to take a portion of the company's contingent compensation, the third party and the amount that party will be entitled to will be mutually approved by the parties. If third parties are approved and entitled to a portion of the companies' contingent compensation, the parties will want to further agree that the third parties' contingent compensation will be deducted "off the top" before the companies receive their respective shares of contingent compensation. Another requirement that the companies may agree to is that each will account to the other in connection with any back-end payments received. In this regard, the companies may further agree to the right to inspect and audit the other company's books and records relating to the accounting statements to verify the accuracy of the others reporting.

(c) Project Ownership. The Parties agree that Company 1 and Company 2 shall be exclusive owners, fifty percent (50%) to Company 1 and fifty percent (50%) to Company 2, in perpetuity and throughout the universe, of all right, title, and interest in and to the Project, including, but not limited to, the title, concept, themes, format, characters, stories, and all other contents thereof, and all translations, adaptations, sequels, and other versions thereof, and in and to the copyright thereof and all renewals and extensions of such copyright, including without limitation the exclusive right to produce and distribute in all media now known or hereafter devised all types of audiovisual works of any kind based upon the Project and allied rights therein (including by way of illustration all soundtrack, music publishing, and merchandising rights).

The companies will generally split ownership of the project on a 50/50 basis if the project is sold. Even though Company 2 brought the idea to Company 1, the expectation is that Company 1 will have contributed additional ideas and helped to develop the project by the time the project is sold. However, once sold, the companies will give up certain ownership rights to the buyer (see Chapter 8). Regardless, it is important that both parties understand that once a network purchases the project, certain ownership rights will be negotiated and sold and the companies will split whatever remains equally.

The parties may negotiate for additional terms for inclusion in the collaboration agreement that will apply if a buyer desires to "set up" the project. Examples include:

Level of Services: During the term the companies generally agree to render reasonable development services on a non-exclusive basis (i.e., the companies can develop other projects with other producers and production companies during the term of the collaboration agreement). A production company could not survive if it were only permitted to shop one project at a time. Just because the company's services are non-exclusive, however, does not mean that the project is also non-exclusive or that either company has the right to create and develop a project similar to the project that the companies are pitching together.

It is also important that both companies understand that once the project is sold, the buyer may request additional exclusivity, which will be defined in the production services agreement. The services can range from exclusive services (i.e., the company will render services on a full-time, exclusive, in-person basis throughout all production periods), non-exclusive services (i.e., the company will render services on a non-exclusive but real, meaningful basis), or passive services (i.e., the company will render services on a non-exclusive, non-in-person passive basis). In this regard, the level of services relate directly to company owners and executives who will likely be named in the collaboration agreement.

Episodic Fees: If the parties do not agree to split the pooled fees (see Paragraph 2(b) above), Company 2 may negotiate for an episodic fee (Company 1 will negotiate its fee when the project is sold directly with the buyer). Company 2's fee will likely be based on the company's precedent, the expected budget of the project, and the level of services the company and its executives intend to render. Examples of how the episodic fees could be structured include:

1. A per-episode fixed fee in the amount of Fifteen Thousand Dollars, if produced for initial exhibition on a broadcast television network (i.e., CBS, NBC, CW, FBC), Ten Thousand Dollars if produced for initial exhibition on cable television, or a fee to be negotiated in good faith if produced for initial exhibition online;

2. An amount equal to five percent of the final buyer-approved episodic budget for the project;

3. If Company 2 renders passive services for the project, then Company 2 shall be paid one third (1/3) of the episodic fee; and

4. An executive producer fee shall be negotiated directly with the network and set forth as a separate line item in the budget.

Travel: Company 2 may set its travel requirements (e.g., air travel, hotel accommodations, ground transportation, and per diem) should their services be required at a distant location. Even though this may be agreed to in the collaboration agreement, the companies will want to qualify that the travel arrangements will be subject to the customary parameters of the buyer with respect to travel and the budget of the project.

Good Faith Negotiation: If the credit, fees, compensation, profit participation, etc. are not negotiated and agreed to in the collaboration agreement, the terms will be subject to good faith negotiation between the companies and the buyer when the project is set-up. The companies may wish to qualify the negotiation as "within the parameter of the budget for the project" or "subject to the company's (and/or company executives') previous quotes for similar services." The parties will want to further agree that neither party will act in a manner that will frustrate the companies' ability to conclude a deal with the buyer or that will unreasonably delay the development and or production of the project.

3. Approvals/Control: All material decisions to be made regarding or concerning the Project shall be by written, unanimous consent by Company 1 and Company 2. Mr./Ms. Executive is the sole representative authorized to provide Company 1's consent and Mr./Ms. Executive is the sole representative authorized to provide Company 2's consent. For these purposes an "email" or similar written digital communication shall constitute "written" communication. It is understood and agreed that if within the Term any development, pilot, special, and/or series based on the Project has been ordered by a Network, then Company 1 and Company 2 shall mutually choose the Showrunner for the Show. It is understood and agreed that during the Term Mr./Ms. Executive 1,

Mr./Ms. Executive 2, and Employee shall each have the right to develop the Project together, such development including, but not limited to, providing opinions, creative feedback, and recommendations on concept, character, art, and all other areas of development and production; assisting in managing creative talent and materials for development and production of the Project and business development; providing opinions, feedback, and recommendations related to sales, marketing, meetings, and potential business deals including sales, licensing, talent, and service work; and attending key internal and external meetings, pitches, service work opportunities, development, and production related meetings, as reasonably required.

Neither Mr./Ms. Executive, Company 1, Mr./Ms. Executive, Company 2, nor Employee has, nor shall any of the foregoing hold himself, herself, or itself out to have, any right, power, or authority to individually create any contract or obligation, either express or implied, on behalf of, in the name of, or binding on the Project.

The Parties agree that each are providing services on a non-exclusive basis and may engage in other film and television activities.

The companies may want to decide or clarify from the outset which company has control over decisions relating to the project. If neither company has absolute control, the companies may require mutual agreement on all decisions. Another solution is to permit Company 2 meaningful consultation or approval, but in the event of a disagreement Company 1's decision will control. This negotiation point will always come down to the bargaining power and experience of each company. In any case, the companies may want to add an additional protection stating that each company shall keep the other informed in a reasonable and timely manner of all matters and decisions regarding the project and further require that each company will respond to communications from the other regarding the project and from others having an interest in the project in a reasonable and timely manner so as not to harm or unreasonably delay the development, production, or exploitation of the project.

The companies may also split the authority to make decisions based on whether the issue is related to a creative choice or a business decision. Creative choices may include decisions relating to the concept, format, casting, hiring of key production personnel (i.e., a showrunner), etc. Business decisions may relate to who the companies pitch the project to, the budget of the project, whether or not to grant profit participation to a third party, etc.

Company 2 will also want to clarify whether or not Company 1 (who is most likely to have the contacts to pitch the project) has the ability to bind Company 2 and/or the project. Generally, either one company has authority or neither company has authority (i.e., neither company can bind the other or the project without express approval) to enter into a contract or create an obligation on behalf of the project and the companies. If both companies are acting on behalf of the project without consulting one another they could subject themselves to conflicting obligations, which could be costly and, even worse, could lead to litigation.

4. Expenses: It is understood and agreed that if within the Term any development, pilot, special, and/or series based on the Project has been ordered by a Network, then Company 1 and Company 2 shall receive reimbursement for all actual out-of-pocket expenses incurred regarding the Project, such reimbursement to be paid first from the budget of any development, pilot, special, and/or series based on the Project that has been ordered by a Network. In order to receive reimbursement, Company 1 and Company 2 must mutually agree in writing to any and all costs and expenses offered for reimbursement. For these purposes an "email" or similar written digital communication shall constitute "in writing."

Both companies will likely incur expenses in developing and shopping the project. Costs in connection with creating a sizzle reel, traveling to pitch the project, hiring production staff, attaching talent, engaging a law firm, etc. can quickly add up and it should be decided at the outset which company will bear the cost and if that company will be reimbursed. The most practical option is to agree to recoup the expenses from the budget once the project is sold. This is a risk to whoever advances these costs. Of course, the project may not sell before the expiration of the term, or the network may not approve the expenses as a line item in the budget. When advising a client, it is important to be forthright and advise that there is always the potential that the expenses may not be recouped and so money spent in the development process should only be done so following careful consideration.

5. Indemnities: See Chapter 2

6. Results and Proceeds: See Chapter 2

> Once the project is sold, the parties will have to give up certain ownership rights in order for a network to produce a show based on the parties' idea. The specifics of what each party must license or convey are negotiated between the buyer and the parties in the Production Services Agreement (see Chapter 8).

7. Reversion: At the end of the Term, if any development, pilot, special, and/or series based on the Project has not been ordered by a Network, then all rights with respect to the Project in addition to the elements thereof granted by the parties (if any) shall revert to Company 2. However, if within one (1) year after the Term the Project is ordered for development, pilot, special, and/or series by a Network that was introduced, involved, engaged, or otherwise put into contact with the Project by Company 1, Mr./Ms. Executive, or Employee during the Term (either directly or indirectly), then Company 1, Mr./Ms. Executive, and Employee will be attached to the Project on the terms set forth in this Agreement.

> Despite the companies' best efforts, the term may expire without interest from a buyer. The companies may have expended a great deal of money and time, so it is important to decide from the outset (1) who will own the initial idea, and (2) who will own the materials created during the term. Generally the company who brought the idea to the collaboration (in this case, "Company 2") will be permitted to proceed with its attempts to "set up" the project without the attachment of the other company (in this case, "Company 1"). Company 1, however, will likely do two things to protect its investment in Company 2's idea. The first is to keep itself "attached" to the project for a defined period of time (generally 3 months to 1 year) if the project is set up following the expiration of the term. This is known as a "tail" or a "sunset period." After the companies agree that there will be a tail and agree to the term of the tail, the companies will next agree whether they will be attached during the tail unconditionally or if selling the

project to certain third-party buyers qualifies Company 1 for continued attachment to the project. Depending on the negotiating power of companies, examples of attachment language may include:

- Company 1 shall be attached if the Project or a project that is similar to Company 2's initial idea is "set up" with a Network.

- Company 1 shall be attached if the Project is "set up" with a Network that was introduced, involved, engaged, or otherwise put into contact with the project by Company 1.

- Company 1 shall be attached if the Project is "set up" with a Network Company 1 submitted the project to during the term.

If Company 2 sells the project, and based on the terms of the collaboration agreement Company 1 remains attached, unless otherwise agreed Company 1 will be attached on the same terms of the collaboration agreement.

If Company 2 has no leverage in the negotiation (i.e., little to no experience in unscripted television and/or no other producers or production companies interested in the project other than Company 1), then Company 2 may also agree that when the term and the "tail" expire Company 1 will receive an executive producer credit and will be further entitled to a per episode royalty and/or a portion of net profits when the project is set up. This clause is perpetual. Ten years from the expiration of the term and the tail, Company 1 will still receive the benefit of the collaboration agreement. When advising Company 2 as to whether or not they should agree to this term, it is important that Company 2 understands that this may inhibit its ability to sell the idea/project in the future when another collaborator or buyer may not want to agree. Company 2 should only agree to this if they have no other options and they absolutely require the expertise and contacts of Company 1.

Company 1 can also protect itself by retaining all rights to the development, pitch, business, and creative materials (e.g., sizzle reel, outlines, ideas, characters, etc.) developed by Company 1 or on Company 1's behalf. Company 2 may request the right to "purchase" the rights back from Company 1 if the project is "set up" with a third party after the expiration of the term and the "tail." If Company 1 agrees to sell the materials it created, Company 1 will usually request reimbursement for the actual, direct, out-of-pocket costs incurred in connection with creating such materials, plus interest. If Company 1 will not agree to sell its materials to Company 2, then Company 2 can only use the concept that they brought to the collaboration and any ideas created without the assistance of Company 1.

It is imperative that the companies decide who will own all the development materials upon the expiration of the term from the outset; otherwise neither company will feel comfortable with proceeding without fear of a lawsuit from the other company claiming rights in and to the idea.

8. Applicable Law: See Chapter 2

9. Assignment: See Chapter 2

10. Miscellaneous: The Parties agree that all provisions and/or terms not discussed herein, which are normally included in similar instruments (e.g., force majeure, limitation of remedies, termination, and suspension) shall be subject to good faith negotiations within customary industry parameters for productions of the type to be produced hereunder.

11. Binding Agreement: Unless and until the Parties enter into a more detailed, formal Agreement, this Agreement shall constitute a binding agreement between the Parties, shall supersede any prior or contemporaneous agreements, and may not be waived or amended, except by a written instrument signed by both Parties. This Agreement may be executed in one or more separate counterparts, each of which, when executed, shall be deemed to be an original. Such counterparts shall, together, constitute and be one and the same agreement.

Very truly yours,

Mr./Ms. Executive

ACCEPTED AND AGREED:

Second Reality TV
Production Company, Inc.

Reality TV
Production Company, Inc.

_____

Mr./Ms. Executive 2,
President

By: _____

Mr./Ms. Executive,
President

DEAL POINT CHECKLIST
Collaboration Agreement

1. Nature and Scope of Relationship
2. Obligations and Contribution of Each Producer
3. Term of the Agreement / Extensions
4. Shopping the Project
   - Exclusivity of the Project
   - Submitting the Project
   - Who Will Attend Pitch Meetings
5. Setting Up the Project
   - Credit
   - Episodic Fee
   - Contingent Compensation
   - Exclusivity / Level of Services
6. Project Ownership
7. Travel
8. Approvals / Control

PART III:

Production

5

Participant Agreement Between a Production Company and an On-Air Participant

"UNTITLED REALITY SHOW" APPLICANT/ PARTICIPANT/RELEASE AGREEMENT

Many reality shows are based on auditioning and selecting individuals who are expected to be themselves on camera. Examples of these types of shows include *The Real World*, *Survivor*, *Big Brother*, and *Fear Factor*, among many other shows. Individuals are expected by producers and production companies to sign an "Applicant/Participant/Release" agreement, most often without negotiating the terms. Potential participants usually do not have negotiating power to obtain any proposed revisions, and most individuals *do* in fact sign the agreement without requesting changes. It is always recommended that an individual engage a qualified person to assist him or her with the decision of whether or not to sign these types of agreements, but it is clear that if an individual does not sign the agreement without changes, then there are many other individuals who will sign the agreement as-is. Therefore, the focus of the comments on this agreement is to explain the extent to which an individual is relinquishing his or her rights, with the understanding that there is little opportunity for individuals to negotiate better terms. The bottom line is that these types of agreements are broad, comprehensive, and require the individual to relinquish many rights. But judging from the number of applicants who sign them, the latter is not a deterrent to those seeking an opportunity to be on television. Once an individual signs the agreement, the best he or she can hope for is that the show becomes a hit in the first or second season; that is, that there are many viewers. If that happens, the participants have created leverage for themselves that may be used to demand renegotiation of the terms in these types of agreements. However, even with the leverage of a successful first or second season, renegotiation is usually limited to the amount each participant is paid for appearing in each episode. Examples of cast members who have banded together, demanded better salary terms, and received substantial pay increases include the participants in the shows *Jersey Shore*, *Deadliest Catch*, *Duck Dynasty*, *Party Down South*, and *Real Housewives of New York*.

The following is a common applicant/participant/release agreement.

INTRODUCTION

I have completed and submitted an application ("Application"), to be considered by Reality Television Production Company, Inc. ("Producer") and/or by Television Network in addition to Network's controlled, controlling, or commonly controlled subsidiaries and affiliates (collectively "Network"), to be a participant in the television series currently entitled Reality Television Series ("Series") which is attached hereto as Exhibit A.

Sometimes the application found within the Participant Agreement, sometimes it is an "Exhibit" attached to the Participant Agreement, and sometimes it is a completely separate document. The application provides the production company with extensive background information on each participant. Examples of some of the information required to be provided by the participant include the following: (1) the participant's employment history for the previous five to ten years; (2) whether or not the applicant was an elected public official, and the promise not to become a candidate for public office for at least one year after broadcast of the last episode that the participant appears; (3) a list of all occurrences in which the participant was detained for or accused of wrongdoing; and (4) a detailed description of arrests, accusations and/or convictions, criminal proceedings, civil lawsuits, and/or restraining orders.

See below for more information about the application.

In consideration of and as an inducement to Producer to continue to consider me to be a participant in the Series, I am making the representations, warranties, disclosures, covenants, and agreements in this applicant/participant/release agreement ("Agreement"). If any representation, warranty, disclosure, covenant, and/or agreement in the Application and/or Agreement is false, misleading, or incomplete, or if I breach any agreement made in connection with the Series, then at any time Producer may remove me from consideration as a participant in the Series and may remove me from the Series.

The participant usually agrees that the producer can also withhold any prizes, awards, money, and/or other benefits as well as demand return of these.

In the event of the latter, Producer and/or Network may, in its sole discretion, make any explanation, announcement, or disclosure.

The participant will remain subject to the confidentiality clause; see below.

I have been interviewed by Producer in its process of selecting participants for the Series and I am under consideration for participating further in the Series, and Producer's obligations are expressly conditioned upon and subject to the following conditions precedent:

(1) Producer's receipt of fully-executed originals; (2) Participant's compliance with all forms and rules required under law including, but not limited to, completing, signing, and delivering to Producer any and all required employment, tax, and immigration forms; and (3) Producer's receipt of any and all required or requested information and documentation.

> The Producer may add other conditions that are required before the Producer will have any obligations to the participant.

I HAVE BEEN GIVEN AMPLE OPPORTUNITY TO READ, AND I HAVE CAREFULLY READ, THIS ENTIRE AGREEMENT. I REPRESENT AND WARRANT THAT I HAVE THE FULL RIGHT, POWER, AND AUTHORITY TO GRANT THE RIGHTS GRANTED IN THIS AGREEMENT. I CERTIFY THAT I HAVE MADE SUCH AN INVESTIGATION OF THE FACTS PERTINENT TO THIS AGREEMENT AND OF ALL THE MATTERS PERTAINING THERETO AS I HAVE DEEMED NECESSARY, THAT I FULLY UNDERSTAND THE CONTENTS OF THIS AGREEMENT, THAT I AM OF SOUND MIND, AND THAT I INTEND TO BE LEGALLY BOUND BY THIS AGREEMENT. I AM AWARE THAT THIS AGREEMENT IS, AMONG OTHER THINGS, A RELEASE OF LIABILITY FOR FUTURE INJURIES AND A CONTRACT BETWEEN MYSELF AND PRODUCER AND/ OR ITS AFFILIATED ORGANIZATIONS, AND/OR THE NETWORK, AND THAT I AM SIGNING THIS AGREEMENT OF MY OWN FREE WILL. ALL STATEMENTS MADE BY ME IN THIS AGREEMENT ARE TRUE. THE NAME GIVEN BELOW IS MY LEGAL NAME. ANY OTHER NAME(S) OR ALIAS(ES) USED BY ME WITHIN THE PAST FIVE YEARS ARE ALSO NOTED BELOW.

This language is often capitalized and bolded because the Producer wants to stop the participant from subsequently arguing that he or she is not bound by the agreement because of legal defenses such the lack of the participant's legal capacity to enter the contract, unconscionability, mistake, or misrepresentation by the Producer.

PARTICIPATION AND ACKNOWLEDGEMENTS

1. If I am selected by Producer and/or Network to be a participant in the Series, I agree to participate as a participant in connection with the production of the Series as and to the extent that Producer and/or Network requires and on such day(s) and time(s) at such location(s) as Producer and/or Network will designate in its/their sole and unilateral discretion, and any such day(s) and/or time(s) and/or location(s) may be changed by Producer and/or Network in its/their sole and unilateral discretion.

Often this Agreement contains an option for the Producer and/or Network. For example, the Producer and/or Network may have the following options: an option to have the individual appear in a pilot episode and/or the first cycle of the Series subject to the terms of this Agreement, and lasting for six months, increased by an additional six months if the Producer and/or Network produces a pilot before the first cycle of the Series; and five or six additional consecutive, dependent, exclusive, and irrevocable options to have the participant appear in the Series, subject to the terms of this Agreement.

The options are usually not negotiable. However, as mentioned above, the actions of the casts on the shows *Jersey Shore* and *Duck Dynasty* are representative examples of what happens when a show provides a network high ratings in the seasons covered by such options. Both casts of the latter shows decided to not film, which put them in breach of the clear language of their agreements. In these situations a network has two choices: it can decide to remove and replace any participant who is in breach of this Agreement, or it can decide that it doesn't want to change the cast that created such high ratings, therefore renegotiating the amount paid each participant per episode.

2. For the time beginning as of the date of this Agreement through the date that is one (1) year following the initial broadcast of the final episode of the cycle of the Series in which I appear (the "Exclusive Hold Period"), I agree to be exclusive to the Producer and Network to participate in "unscripted/reality-based" programming in which I appear as myself.

> Often the Agreement specifically adds that the participant agrees to participate in further interviews, "reunions," "making of," or other "special programs," and the term length may extend from one (1) to three (3) years.

During the Exclusive Hold Period I agree that I shall not grant any interview to any third party without Producer and/or Network's prior written approval.

> Often the Agreement includes terms that broaden the scope of activities subject to prior written approval by the Producer and/or Network. For example, the participant may be required to inform the Producer and/or Network of all third-party offers to provide services in non-reality projects such as scripted projects in any and all media (television, feature films, commercials, media, print, and internet). Such third-party offers would be subject to approval by the Producer and/or Network in its/their unilateral and sole discretion. The participant should try to carve out an exception that such approval is not necessary if such services are provided to the Network, or any station or website owned by the Network.

(a) During the Exclusive Hold period I agree to be available and to participate as and where Producer and/or Network may require in connection with publicity, interviews, promotion, marketing, advertising, and other matters in connection with the Series or otherwise. Without limiting the foregoing, I agree to appear on news shows, morning shows, talk shows, in-store events, press tours, including but not limited to Upfronts, and to make other appearances as required by the Producer and/or

Network. Without limiting the foregoing, I agree to give on- or off-set interviews to such parties as Producer and/or Network shall request, including, without limitation, the publicist for the Series, newspaper journalists, magazine, television, radio, internet, or otherwise. There shall not be any additional compensation for any of the above-referenced activities.

> The individual would like to request transportation, accommodations, and a per diem, but the lack of negotiating power will probably result in the rejection of such a request. The individual will have to get himself or herself to these events and provide accommodations if the production company doesn't arrange them. Even if the production company does provide these necessities, the individual should expect the least expensive options to be provided.

(b) During the Exclusive Hold period I agree to pose for still photographs, and be available and participate in screen tests, post-production consultations, recording sessions, videotaped interviews, and any other activity that Producer and/or Network may request in its/their sole discretion.

> The Producer/Network often requires the participant to try to have family members, co-workers, and friends participate in the videotaped interviews and other activities.

There shall not be any additional compensation for any of the above-referenced activities.

3. I acknowledge and agree that I may be chosen as an alternate (that is, not as a "participant") by Producer and/or Network in its/their sole discretion. If I am chosen as an alternate I shall remain available to participate in the Series as a "participant" if and when chosen as a replacement for another participant. I understand and acknowledge that if I am chosen as an alternate and not chosen to replace a participant, then

I do not have any chance to participate in the Series or receive any consideration of any kind, monetary or otherwise. I acknowledge and agree that Producer and/or Network have the right at any time and in its/their sole discretion to add, remove, or replace participants.

> Each reality show will have its own rules regarding any prizes or awards that a participant can obtain. If an alternate is chosen as a participant for any reason, the manner in which any such prizes, awards, or other benefits are impacted by such change will be found in this paragraph.

I acknowledge and agree that all the terms and conditions of this Agreement shall apply to me with full force and effect whether I am initially selected as an alternate or a participant.

4. I understand that I may discontinue my participation in the Series and withdraw as an alternate, potential, or actual participant in the Series at any time, provided, however, that my withdrawal, discontinuation, or other refusal to participate will affect any of the rights assigned by me, or any of the covenants, agreements, waivers, releases, or indemnities made by me in this Agreement. If I voluntarily withdraw from the Series I shall forfeit any consideration to which I otherwise would have been entitled, and shall be required to return any consideration already received in connection with the Series.

> Although the participant can leave a show, he or she is agreeing that any and all money, goods, or other valuable items that he or she has received must be returned to the Producer.

Producer and/or Network may require any withdrawal to occur on camera and be recorded, and that any Material obtained by Producer and/or Network prior to withdrawal and any Material relating to any such withdrawal may be exploited by Producer and/or Network as part of the Series or otherwise.

The participant leaving the show may *not* be allowed to leave quietly, since the Producer has the right to require him or her to withdraw from the show on camera. Further, the Producer has the right to use any footage already captured in any manner.

I acknowledge and agree that my voluntary withdrawal from the Series and/or my taking any action rendering me ineligible or otherwise unable to participate in the Series will not relieve me of my obligation to stay in a location designated by Producer and/or Network in its/their sole discretion under Producer's/Network's supervision until completion of production of the Series.

Even if a participant withdraws, makes himself or herself ineligible, or is unable to participate, the producer retains the right *to require* the participant to stay in any location chosen by the Producer, and remain under the Producer's supervision, until the end of the show. Once a participant agrees to be in a show, he or she will not be able to return to his or her normal life until the end of the show. This can be an onerous requirement, and is certainly an incentive *not* to leave a show once it has begun filming.

I will disclose to Producer and/or Network if any friend, relative, or acquaintance appears in the series and I understand that in such event I can be disqualified as a participant at the sole and absolute discretion of Producer and/or Network. I acknowledge and agree that if I should voluntarily discontinue my participation in the Series and/or take any action that would render me ineligible to participate in the Series or if I am disqualified for any reason at any time after the execution of this Agreement, Producer and Network would suffer significant cost and expense as a result of such discontinuation and/or action. I understand and agree that proof of such damages will be costly, difficult, and inconvenient. Accordingly, I agree to pay Producer and Network each the sum of Fifty Thousand Dollars ($50,000.00) as liquidated damages if I voluntarily discontinue my participation in the Series and/or take any action that would render me ineligible to participate in the Series at any time after the execution of this Agreement for any reason other than concern for my physical safety, extreme personal emergency, or any similar event beyond my control.

An additional incentive not to do anything contrary to the rules of the show or to simply voluntarily discontinue participation is that the participant agrees to pay $50,000 if he or she voluntarily discontinues. There are three exceptions to this, but each one would require the participant to prove the existence of such events that are subject to interpretation. That is, what constitutes concern for physical safety, extreme personal emergency, or an event beyond the participant's control would most likely require the participant to engage an attorney to negotiate and convince the Producer that such event exists and the participant should therefore not be required to pay the $50,000.

I agree that Fifty Thousand Dollars ($50,000.00) is a reasonable amount of damages Producer and Network are each likely to suffer, considering all of the circumstances existing as of the date of this Agreement.

5. I acknowledge and understand that:

   (a) I am freely and knowingly consenting to the filming, taping, audio, and other recording of me in connection with the Series that could otherwise constitute a serious actionable invasion of my privacy;

Note the phrase "serious actionable invasion of privacy." The participant is acknowledging that the Producer has the right to engage in actions toward the participant that otherwise would require the Producer to be responsible for the damages created by the Producer's actions. Some examples of the invasion of individual's privacy by filming, taping, or audio include: (a) filming in otherwise private areas such as home, bedroom or bathroom; (b) revealing private facts of a person such as sexual history and preferences, hygiene, illnesses, and family history; and (c) fabricating events and facts and attributing them to a person. A "serious actionable invasion of privacy" also includes the use of photos or film to imply statements as fact regarding an individual although they are untrue.

(b) I understand that film, tape, audio, and other recording of my actions and statements and devices placed where I am located in connection with the Series may be made using concealed or hidden devices and I expressly agree and consent to such recordings made using concealed devices;

Each reality show will add different places that may be specific to that show, for example, recording devices in the phones, shower/bathrooms, bedrooms, cars, and personal items.

(c) I give my express, unconditional, and irrevocable permission to Producer and Network to fully exploit all materials made using any type of recording device (which are "Material" under the Grant of Rights in this Agreement) whether or not my privacy has been or will be invaded by making or exhibiting such material and whether or not such materials violate any other rights I now hold or may hold in the future;

A clear statement that the participant is allowing the Producer to use the materials obtained by violating the person's privacy.

(d) I may reveal and/or relate, and other parties (including, but not limited to, Producer, any employee or independent contractor of the Producer and/or Network, and other participants) may reveal and/or relate information about me of a personal, private, intimate, surprising, defamatory, disparaging, embarrassing, or unfavorable nature, and that the actions of others appearing in the Series may be embarrassing or of an otherwise unfavorable nature that may be factual or fictional;

Defamatory actions are actions that hurt someone's reputation. If the action is said then it is slander; if the action is written or published then it is defamation. The participant is agreeing that the Producer has the right to slander and defame the participant, in addition to the right of the Producer to take actions that disparage or embarrass him or her.

(e) my appearance, depiction, and/or portrayal in and in connection with the Series (including, but not limited to, the title of the Series), and my actions and the actions of others displayed in and in connection with the Series may be disparaging, defamatory, embarrassing, or of an otherwise unfavorable nature, may expose me to public ridicule, humiliation, or condemnation, and may portray me in a false light;

Defamatory actions are actions that hurt someone's reputation. If the action is said then it is slander; if the action is written or published then it is defamation. The participant is agreeing that the Producer has the right to slander and defame the participant, in addition to the right of the Producer to take actions that disparage or embarrass him or her.

(f) I hereby freely and knowingly consent to the following conduct that might otherwise constitute an actionable tort:

Each reality show will expose its participants to different types of conduct and it is generally described in this sub-paragraph. For example, the Agreement may state that the Producer and/or Network may in its/their sole discretion require the participant to wear certain costumes, clothing, accessories, and makeup. The Producer and/or Network may disclose and disseminate negative information about the participant. They also are allowed to disclose some information that is more or less favorable than information disclosed or disseminated about other participants.

(g) Producer and/or Network may make misrepresentations to me and others for dramatic or any other purpose. Such misrepresentations may relate to any and all topics of every kind and nature.

> For example, some of the allowable misrepresentations can be about other participants, the title of the show, information the producer provides about the show or other participants, events, the status of the participant in the show, whether any consideration or benefit exists or will be provided to the participant, and conditions applicable to the participant's potential or actual participation in the show.

I hereby freely and knowingly consent to such conduct although I understand and acknowledge that such conduct might otherwise constitute an actionable tort. The waivers, releases, and indemnities in this Agreement and any other agreement that I have executed or that I may execute in connection with the Series expressly apply to such actions described in this paragraph;

(h) I will not infringe or violate the rights of any other person or entity. I shall not cause injury or harm to the person or property of any other person. I will abide by all participant rules of conduct; US federal, state, and local laws, rules, regulations, codes, and ordinances; and the laws, rules, regulations, codes, and ordinances in effect in any location I visit outside the US;

(i) I will not commit any act which adversely affects my public image, my ability to perform my duties and obligations under this Agreement, and/or the Producer's and/or Network's public image;

(j) I will not intimidate with threats of physical violence or bodily harm against any other actual or potential participant in the

Series, any employees, independent contractors, agents, or other representatives of Producer and/or Network, or against any other person or party. I will not cause any physical injury or physical harm to any other actual or potential participant in the Series, any employees, independent contractors, agents, or other representatives of Producer and/or Network, or to any other person or party. COMPLETE ADHERENCE TO THIS PARAGRAPH IS OF ESSENCE TO THIS AGREEMENT. Any breach may result in immediate termination of my actual or potential participation in the Series with no further obligation to me whatsoever. The waivers, releases, and indemnities in this Agreement and any other agreement that I have executed or that I may execute in connection with the Series expressly apply to any criminal or civil penalties that may be imposed on me, and to any disqualification of me by Producer and/or Network;

The participant is placed on notice regarding certain actions that are not allowed while participating in the show. The Producer will often be held liable for the damages caused by a participant in the show, but these paragraphs preclude a participant from claiming that he or she was not aware that such actions were prohibited. In addition, these terms evidence that the Producer has taken appropriate steps to properly inform the participant of the limitations. There have been a number of incidents on reality shows where a participant has engaged in physical intimidation or violence toward a fellow participant or other third parties. It should be noted that it states that such actions *may* result in termination from participation in the series. There have been examples where the producers of a show immediately removed a participant who engaged in violence; for example, on *The Real World*, and other times where a participant was not removed from the show; for example, incidents where participants in the show *Jersey Shore* engaged in fistfights with third parties or actions between a man and a woman involved in a personal relationship could possibly be determined to be domestic violence. The language in these agreements clearly states that the Producer has the unilateral power to decide what consequences will result from such actions with regards to the show.

(k) I will not damage any equipment, wardrobe, or other materials furnished and/or used by Producer and/or Network in connection with the production of the Series. I will not tamper with or hinder the equipment used for purposes of recording the Series.

(l) I will not enter into any personal and/or social relationships with any of the Producer's or Network's employees, independent contractors, agents, or other representatives of Producer and/or Network, or any individual closely related to the production of the Series. Any breach may result in immediate termination of my actual or potential participation in the Series with no further obligation to me whatsoever.

A Producer may not have a problem with participants engaging in personal relationships with other participants because it may increase ratings for the show. However, the Producer in this Agreement has determined that relationships between participants and employees, independent contractors, agents, or other representatives who *are not* contractually obligated to be on camera and *may not* have agreed to waive certain legal rights, as the participants do, will only cause problems for the Producer. Therefore, it is prohibited by the Producer.

The following terms are usually added to the Agreement and they are most commonly non-negotiable. However, if a participant has leverage and a producer and/or network wants to have him or her on the show, then the participant may be able to obtain more favorable terms. For example, individuals who have a talent that will be utilized in a show, such as a professional skateboarder, professional BMX rider, professional dancer, or other individuals who are less replaceable than a general reality show participant. In any case, the common terms the participant agrees to include the following: 1) Travel. If the participant is required to travel for the Series then the Producer should provide reasonable transportation; 2) Accommodations. If the participant is required to travel for the Series then the Producer should provide reasonable accommodations. Often the room must be shared with other participants. Incidental expenses (phone, food, mini-bar, television, wireless internet, etc.) will be the responsibility of the participant. 3) A per diem payment is not usually provided for a participant. A per diem is a small amount of money, usually between twenty-five and one hundred dollars, that an individual receives from the producer for daily expenses.

The participant may want to negotiate for an all-inclusive amount for travel and accommodations. In any case, all other expenses incurred and not covered in the Agreement will be the responsibility of the participant. However, the Producer will often provide the least expensive options necessary to make sure the participant is available to provide on-camera services.

RULES

If I am selected as a participant, I understand that I will be provided a copy of the Series rules ("Series Rules").

Generally, the Series Rules are attached as an Exhibit to the Agreement, are often of a length between one and six pages, and are specifically drafted for each reality show.

I agree to read, follow, and obey the Series Rules (as they may be changed, modified, or amended by Producer and/or Network in its/their sole discretion from time to time, with or without notice to me). I agree to cooperate with, follow, and obey all reasonable and lawful rules, instructions, and directions of Producer and the Network in connection with the Series. I will immediately report to Producer any violations of the Series Rules by any individual, including myself. I understand that my failure to comply with any of the Series Rules in any respect or to any degree may result in the Producer's sole, unilateral determination to immediately disqualify and/or eliminate me from the Series and also require forfeiture of any and all prizes, stipends, or other monies or benefit even if any of the latter have already been promised to or received by me. Producer's and/or Network's decisions in any and all matters (including but not limited to the following: participant selection and elimination; the creation and interpretation of any term, condition, and rule; and the actions of producer and/or Network for any failure to comply with any rule, instruction, or direction) shall be with Producer's and/or Network's control and shall be final and binding on me in all respects and shall not be subject to challenge or appeal. If any activity regarding the Series is stopped for any reason, I will abide by the Producer's and/or Network's decision regarding the resumption of the activity and the disposition of any prize, stipend, money, or any other benefit promised, provided, or otherwise promised to be available. I understand that the Producer reserves the right in its sole discretion and at any time (whether before, during, or after production) to change, alter, add to, amend, delete from, or modify the Series Rules or any of the terms and/or conditions regarding the Series, including, but not limited to, those affecting or governing the conduct of the participants on the Series, the Series activities, the elimination of participants for the Series, and the granting and withholding of any prize, stipend, money, or any other benefit promised, provided or otherwise promised to be available.

CONSENTS AND AUTHORIZATIONS

> Generally, each Agreement will have a basic group of terms that each participant will agree to, but the following five groupings are found in most participant agreements. However, they may be augmented with language that is applicable to a specific show.

Group 1: Physical. The participant will represent and warrant that he or she is in excellent physical, emotional, and mental condition and he or she is able to engage in the activities of the show. The participant also represents and warrants that he or she does not have any sexually transmitted diseases (STDs) and acknowledges that other participants may have STDs and that the participant engages in sex at his or her own risk—although the Producer and Network specifically disclaim any requirement or encouragement of such actions.

Group 2: Privacy Waivers. The participant authorizes the Producer and Network to investigate, access, and collect information from anyone, including current and former employers, roommates, spouses, boyfriends, girlfriends, family members, co-workers, educational institutions, government entities, employment records, medical records, criminal records, motor vehicle records, and credit records. The participant also authorizes the Producer and Network to use such information. Some shows state the information can be used for any purpose in choosing participants; other shows state that the information can be used for any purpose at Producer's and Network's sole and unilateral discretion.

Group 3: Access To Locations. The participant authorizes the Producer and Network to enter any and all areas of participant's residence(s) and work. The Producer and/or Network are authorized to obtain information, take pictures and photographs, make recordings, and take any material found at these locations, with the promise to return the materials when the participant finishes filming for the show.

Group 4: Permitted Items. The participant promises not to bring illegal drugs, dangerous or wild animals, weapons of any kind, guns and knives of any kind, and this list can often be much longer. Many shows also state a list of items that may not be permitted such as vitamins, food and beverages of any kind, etc. The participant consents to search of the participant and his or her possessions at any time and agrees that anything confiscated will not be returned.

Group 5: Medical. The participant agrees to drug testing and testing for sexually transmitted diseases as often as demanded by the Producer and Network. If the participant gets sick, he or she authorizes the Producer and/or Network to arrange for or provide medical assistance in its/their sole discretion. The participant waives any confidentiality between the participant and any and all medical providers.

The participant unconditionally and irrevocably releases the Producer and Network from liability regarding all of the consents and authorizations participant provided in the Agreement. Further, the participant agrees that the Producer and Network can remove the participant from the show for any reason.

PARTICIPANT APPLICATION

Each show has an application that is often inserted in the body of this Agreement; sometimes it is attached as an exhibit to the Agreement or may be its own separate agreement. Each show drafts the questions to address the specific concerns raised by the show, but there are many questions a participant is required to answer that are common to all participant applications. The following addresses many of the common questions.

The first group of applicant questions ask about the prospective participant's background. Questions cover: (a) the prospective participant's age, citizenship, and marital status; (b) whether or not he or she is or will be a candidate for public office; (c) what other television shows he or she has applied for or appeared on; (d) whether or not he or she is a member of any guild: for example, Screen Actors Guild-American Federation of Television and Radio Artists; (e) his or her criminal background, including arrests, accusations, and convictions; civil and criminal proceedings he or she has been involved in; (f) military background, including honorable or dishonorable discharge; (g) anything he or she has been involved in that may reflect negatively on the show, producers, and/or network; (h) any professional training; (i) whether he or she has posed nude or semi-nude or has performed sexual acts in any media.

The second group of applicant questions are in the form of the prospective applicant representing and warranting that he or she: (a) has no knowledge or access to any material, challenges, assignments, or competitions, or access to anyone who has access to the latter show elements; (b) will not display any trademark or brand on air; (c) will not "plug" any service, product, or other venture on air; (d) has provided all true and accurate statements, disclosures, and representations; (e) understands and agrees that any and all statements, disclosures, and representations can be disclosed to anyone by any means, whether on or off camera.

The third group of questions asks the prospective participant to state that he or she understands and agrees that he or she is responsible for all taxes relating to any benefit received from participating in the show and that he or she is also responsible for any and all costs associated with receiving any benefit from participating in the show, such as shipping, insurance, and similar costs.

Richard Hatch, the first winner of the $1 million prize on the show *Survivor,* was found guilty of failing to pay federal income taxes on his winnings and was sentenced to three years in prison. He attempted to claim in his proceedings that the producers of the show were required to pay the taxes. The producers denied his claim and provided the terms of this clause to support their position.

GRANT OF RIGHTS

See Chapter 2.

Participant agreements often add terms specific to this type of agreement, including the following: (a) the right to interview the participant for as many times and however long a producer wants and the right to videotape, film, or otherwise record such interviews; (b) a producer's right to own all ideas, gags, suggestions, themes, plots, stories, characters, characterizations, dialogue, text, designs, graphics, titles, drawings, choreography, artwork, digital works, songs, music, photography, video, film, and other material, whether or not fixed or reduced to drawing or writing, at any time created or contributed by the participant which in any way relate to the show; (c) the participant's appearance, actions, voice, and sound effects in connection with the show (including, but not limited to, any act, poses, plays, vocal, instrumental, musical, and other sound effects), compositions of any kind or nature, and the results and proceeds of the individual's participation in the show, and any reproductions or recordings of any nature; (d) all copyrights, trademarks, and ownership of any other rights. For example, Mike "The Situation" Sorrentino, a participant on the show *Jersey Shore*, tried to obtain a trademark for certain "catchphrases" from the show such as "GTL" ("gym, tan, laundry"). However, the producer filed a claim stopping him because it stated it is the owner of such catchphrases, citing this language from the participant agreement that Sorrentino had signed; (e) the right to use the participant's name, likeness (actual or simulated), photograph, caricature, voice, and biographical material for any commercial purpose whatsoever, including but not limited to product endorsement. A reality television participant has none of the following safeguards that well-known actors can obtain. Well-known actors specifically negotiate and usually receive agreement that their name and likeness shall not be used to endorse any product. If they do agree to allow their name and likeness to endorse a product, they negotiate and *receive payment* in addition to agreeing to certain products that the producer is prohibited from using the name and likeness for, such as the following: the producer will agree not to use the well-known actor's name and likeness or exploit or otherwise publicly display in connection with the merchandising of, or commercial tie-ins, for the following categories: gambling, religious, political, alcohol, tobacco, drugs (prescription or non-prescription), firearms (including toy versions thereof), undergarments, feminine or personal hygiene, pornography, or sexually explicit; and (f) participants on shows such as *Project Runway* and *So You Think You Can Dance* will be required to agree that any and all material created or displayed will be subject to the Producer's approval, will not be subject to any third party's rights, and will meet nationwide public standards of decency and shall not be deemed inappropriate by a reasonable person. In some situations the participant also agrees that the artistic material created in connection with the show—for example, songs, skits, choreography, and music—are owned by the Producer.

LIFE STORY RIGHTS

Contingent upon my selection as a participant in the Series, I hereby irrevocably grant and release to Producer and Network, in perpetuity and throughout the universe, the exclusive right to depict, portray, and represent me and my life and all episodes, exploits, events, incidents, situations, and experiences contained in or associated or related to my life which occur, will occur, or have occurred at any time (including, without limitation, my experiences in connection with the Series) (my "Life Story") . . . in any and all media, whether now known or hereafter devised, and in the exercise of all subsidiary, allied, and ancillary rights (e.g., remake, sequel, theatrical, television, radio, publishing, merchandising, soundtrack album, and other similar rights).

> A participant who signs this Agreement allows the production company to tell any and all stories about the participant's life. The rights include not only things that have happened or are happening, but things that *will happen* in the future. The participant not only gives away the rights to tell his or life story; the next paragraph allows the production company extraordinary freedom in telling the participant's story.

Producer and/or the Network may depict, portray, and represent me and my Life Story either accurately or with such liberties and modifications as Producer and/or the Network determines necessary or desirable in its/their sole discretion for the purposes of fictionalization, dramatization, or any other purposes, including, without limitation, to achieve a humorous or satirical effect, and by means of actors who may or may not resemble me.

> The participant agrees to allow the production company to fictionalize and misrepresent the participant's life story in any manner.

Contingent upon my selection as a participant in the Series, I hereby agree that I shall obtain, for no additional cost to Producer and/or Network, releases from members of my immediate family, which shall include, without limitation, my spouse, or spousal equivalent, life partner, mother, stepmother(s), father, stepfather(s), girlfriend(s), boyfriend(s), daughter(s), son(s), sister(s), brother(s), roommate(s), and any other person who resides in my home or with me, who may appear on camera or whom I may discuss or make reference to on camera, and any other person Producer and/or Network may designate, such release(s) to be in a form designated and provided by Producer and/or Network.

> The participant is expected to obtain releases from all of the individuals the participant speaks with or about. These individuals are not required to provide their permission or release, so these are terms that can place the participant in breach of this Agreement.

Contingent upon my selection as a participant in the Series, I hereby agree that I shall use my best efforts to obtain, for no additional cost to Producer and/or Network, releases from any other person(s) that Producer and/or Network deems necessary or desirable, such release(s) to be in a form designated and provided by Producer and/or Network.

ASSUMPTION OF RISK

> Assumption of risk, waiver, and releases (collectively "Releases") provide that the participant understands and agrees that he or she will not be able to obtain compensation for injuries that result from the situations in which the participant will be involved on the show. These express Releases in essence relieve the other party (i.e., the production company, network, etc.) of any liability that arises from the specific risks addressed in an agreement. It is very difficult, some may argue that it is near to impossible, to bring a successful action for damages when the party claiming the damages has signed an express Release. It should be noted that it is not a valid defense to claim that the individual signed the express Release without reading it.
>
> The law generally requires that these types of Releases be expressed in clear, unambiguous, detailed language that leaves no room for doubt regarding the intent of the parties signing such a Release. Therefore, the scope of the activities and possible bad outcomes found in the Releases for reality shows are usually broad and specific. For example, the participant will state that he or she will reside in close quarters with other people who may have a disease, be sick, and/or have some other health condition, including, but not limited to, sexually transmitted diseases. The participant further agrees that the production company will not test anyone for any health conditions, the participant assumes all risks, and he or she releases liability for any disease or health condition that he or she contracts.

Each reality show will also specifically state certain activities that the participant will engage in for each show that could lead to injury or death. For example, the participant will acknowledge and consent to participate in activities such as eating items that could make him or her sick or die (participants on the reality show *Fear Factor* have eaten cow bile, rancid cheese, and cave-dwelling spiders), jumping from heights, riding ziplines, swimming, skydiving, racing cars and motorcycles, skateboarding stunts, ice skating, dancing, and other activities.

I AM AWARE THAT THE ACTIVITIES IN WHICH I MAY PARTICIPATE IN CONNECTION WITH THE SERIES (INCLUDING, WITHOUT LIMITATION, THE PARTICIPANT SELECTION PROCESS) MAY BE STRENUOUS, HAZARDOUS, AND/OR DANGEROUS PHYSICAL AND/OR MENTAL ACTIVITIES (WHICH INCLUDE, BUT ARE NOT LIMITED TO: TRAVEL BY AIR, HELICOPTER, COMMERCIAL AIRLINER, PRIVATE AIRCRAFT, OR OTHERWISE: TRAVEL BY AUTOMOBILE, SCOOTER, ALL-TERRAIN VEHICLE, BOAT, TRAIN, AND/OR ANY OTHER VEHICLE; AND I AM VOLUNTARILY PARTICIPATING IN THE SERIES AND RELATED ACTIVITIES WITH FULL KNOWLEDGE, APPRECIATION, AND UNDERSTANDING OF THE DANGERS AND PERSONAL RISKS INVOLVED AND HEREBY AGREE TO ACCEPT ANY AND ALL RISKS OF PARTICIPATING IN CONTESTANT SELECTION AND/OR IN THE SERIES, INCLUDING BUT NOT LIMITED TO ILLNESS, SERIOUS PERSONAL INJURY, NON-CONSENSUAL PHYSICAL CONTACT, DEATH, AND/OR PROPERTY LOSS. FURTHER, I UNDERSTAND AND ACKNOWLEDGE THAT, WHILE CONDUCT GIVING RISE TO SUCH SITUATIONS MIGHT OTHERWISE CONSTITUTE AN ACTIONABLE TORT, I HAVE FREELY AND KNOWINGLY CONSENTED TO SUCH CONDUCT.

I ACKNOWLEDGE THAT NO REPRESENTATIONS OR WARRANTIES OF ANY KIND WHATSOEVER HAVE BEEN MADE TO ME BY PRODUCER REGARDING MY QUALIFICATIONS OR ABILITY TO PARTICIPATE IN THE SERIES, OR REGARDING ANY OF THE EQUIPMENT OR SERVICES TO BE USED IN CONNECTION WITH THE SERIES BY ME OR OTHER PARTICIPANTS, AND I ACKNOWLEDGE AND AGREE THAT I WILL USE THE EQUIPMENT AND SERVICES ENTIRELY AT MY OWN RISK.

RELEASES AND WAIVERS

AS USED IN THIS AGREEMENT, THE TERM "RELEASING PARTIES" MEANS AND REFERS TO EACH OF ME, MY HEIRS, NEXT OF KIN, SPOUSE, SPOUSAL EQUIVALENT, GUARDIANS, LEGAL REPRESENTATIVES, EXECUTORS, ADMINISTRATORS, SUCCESSORS AND ASSIGNS; AND AS USED IN THIS AGREEMENT, THE TERM "RELEASED PARTIES" MEANS AND REFERS TO PRODUCER, NETWORK, NETWORK SUBSIDIARY, ALL TELEVISION STATIONS AND CHANNELS, CABLE NETWORKS, AND SATELLITE NETWORKS THAT BROADCAST OR OTHERWISE EXHIBIT THE SERIES, ALL OTHER PARTICIPANTS IN THE SERIES, ALL SPONSORS AND ADVERTISERS CONNECTED WITH THE SERIES, ALL OTHER PERSONS AND ENTITIES CONNECTED WITH THE SERIES, AND ALL OF THEIR RESPECTIVE PARENTS, SUBSIDIARIES, RELATED AND AFFILIATED COMPANIES, LICENSEES, SPONSORS, SUCCESSORS AND ASSIGNS, AND THE DIRECTORS, OFFICERS, EMPLOYEES, AGENTS, CONTRACTORS, PARTNERS,

SHAREHOLDERS, REPRESENTATIVES, AND MEMBERS OF EACH OF THE FOREGOING ENTITIES, AND THE HEIRS, NEXT OF KIN, SPOUSES, GUARDIANS, LEGAL REPRESENTATIVES, EXECUTORS, ADMINISTRATORS, LICENSEES, SUCCESSORS AND ASSIGNS OF EACH OF THE FOREGOING.

The participant includes family members and other parties that could sue on his or her behalf as parties that are also releasing the other parties from liability. The list of "other parties" that the participant agrees not to hold liable for any injury or death is obviously extensive; it includes the primary parties who are involved with the show and other parties who are involved with those primary parties, such as licensees, sponsors, other companies, and participants.

TO THE MAXIMUM EXTENT PERMITTED BY LAW, THE RELEASING PARTIES AND I HEREBY UNCONDITIONALLY AND IRREVOCABLY AGREE THAT I AND THE OTHER RELEASING PARTIES WILL NOT SUE OR ASSERT ANY CLAIM AGAINST ANY OF THE PARTICIPANTS IN THE SERIES, OR ANY OF THEIR HEIRS, NEXT OF KIN, SPOUSES, SPOUSAL EQUIVALENTS, GUARDIANS, LEGAL REPRESENTATIVES, EXECUTORS, ADMINISTRATORS, SUCCESSORS AND ASSIGNS, OR ANY OF THE OTHER RELEASED PARTIES, AND <u>WILL NOT FILE ANY CLAIM OR COMPLAINT WITH THE AUTHORITIES, INCLUDING BUT NOT LIMITED TO THE FCC, OR INITIATE ANY PROCEEDING, COMPLAINT, OR CLAIM FOR OR IN CONNECTION WITH ANY INJURY, ILLNESS, DAMAGE, EMOTIONAL DISTRESS, LOSS, OR HARM TO ME OR MY PROPERTY, OR MY DEATH, OR ANY INJURY, ILLNESS, DAMAGE, LOSS, OR HARM TO ANY RELEASING PARTIES OR ANY THIRD PARTIES</u>

OR ANY OF THEIR PROPERTY, OR THE DEATH OF
ANY RELEASING PARTIES OR ANY THIRD PARTIES,
HOWSOEVER CAUSED, RESULTING FROM OR ARIS-
ING OUT OF OR IN CONNECTION WITH ANY FRAUD,
INTENTIONAL MISREPRESENTATION, ANY DEFECT
IN AND/OR FAILURE OF EQUIPMENT, WARNINGS OR
INSTRUCTIONS, OR MY APPLICATION OR PREPA-
RATION FOR, PARTICIPATION OR APPEARANCE IN,
OR ELIMINATION FROM THE SERIES OR ACTIVITIES
ASSOCIATED WITH THE SERIES, ANY MISREPRESEN-
TATIONS REGARDING THE PRIZE OR RULES OR CON-
DITIONS FOR WINNING THE PRIZE, OR ANY PRIZE
THAT MAY BE AWARDED, OR ANY OTHER BENEFIT,
WHETHER OCURRING BEFORE, DURING OR AFTER
MY ACTUAL PARTICIPATION IN THE SERIES, AND
WHETHER OR NOT CAUSED BY OR ARISING OUT OF
THE NEGLIGENCE OR GROSS NEGLIGENCE OF ANY
OF THE RELEASED PARTIES OR ANY OF THE PARTIC-
IPANTS IN THE SERIES.

> The participant agrees to allow the "released parties," (i.e., the production company, network, etc.) to also be free from claims and free from responsibility regarding any damages even if the injury, damages, or death are the direct result of gross negligence by the released parties, including but not limited to actions such as fraud, negligence, and intentional misrepresentation by those released parties.

TO THE MAXIMUM EXTENT PERMITTED BY LAW, THE
RELEASING PARTIES AND I HEREBY UNCONDITION-
ALLY AND IRREVOCABLY RELEASE THE RELEASED
PARTIES, AND EACH OF THEM, FROM ANY AND ALL
CLAIMS, ACTIONS, DAMAGES, LIABILITIES, LOSSES,
COSTS, AND EXPENSES OF ANY KIND (INCLUDING,

WITHOUT LIMITATION, ATTORNEYS' FEES AND COSTS) THAT WE MAY NOW HAVE OR MAY HEREAFTER HAVE ARISING OUT OF, RESULTING FROM, OR BY REASON OF MY PARTICIPATION ON OR IN CONNECTION WITH THE SERIES, OR MY APPEARANCE ON THE SERIES, THE FAILURE OF PRODUCER TO SELECT ME AS A CONTESTANT, THE CANCELLATION OF THE SERIES, OR THE EXERCISE BY PRODUCER OR ANYONE ELSE OF ANY RIGHTS GRANTED BY ME UNDER THIS AGREEMENT, INCLUDING, BUT NOT LIMITED TO, ANY CLAIMS FOR LIBEL, SLANDER, DEFAMATION, INVASION OF ANY RIGHTS OF PRIVACY, VIOLATION OF ANY RIGHTS OF PUBLICITY OR PERSONALITY, FALSE LIGHT, INFRINGEMENT OF COPYRIGHT, OR VIOLATION OF ANY OTHER RIGHT. THE RELEASED CLAIMS SPECIFICALLY INCLUDE ANY CLAIMS, ACTIONS, DAMAGES, LIABILITIES, LOSSES, COSTS, AND EXPENSES OF ANY KIND RESULTING FROM THE ACTIONS OF ANOTHER CONTESTANT OR ANY OTHER THIRD PARTY AT ANY TIME, OR FROM ANY DEFECT IN OR FAILURE OF EQUIPMENT, WARNINGS, OR INSTRUCTIONS, OR MY APPLICATION OR PREPARATION FOR, PARTICIPATION OR APPEARANCE IN, OR ELIMINATION FROM THE SERIES, OR ACTIVITIES ASSOCIATED WITH THE SERIES, WHETHER OCCURRING BEFORE, DURING, OR AFTER MY ACTUAL PARTICIPATION IN THE SERIES, AND WHETHER OR NOT CAUSED BY OR ARISING OUT OF THE NEGLIGENCE OR GROSS NEGLIGENCE OF ANY OF THE RELEASED PARTIES.

> The participant further agrees to allow the "released parties," (i.e., the production company, network, etc.) to also be free from any claims and free from any responsibility regarding any damages even if the injury, damages, or death are the direct result of participating in the show, or the failure of the released parties to choose the participant for the show, cancellation of the show, and elimination from the show. In addition, there are specific legal claims the participant agrees not to seek damages for, including libel, slander, and defamation.

INDEMNIFICATION

See Chapter 2.

REPRESENTATIONS AND WARRANTIES

See Chapter 2.

CONFIDENTIALITY

> Sometimes a separate Confidentiality and Non-Disclosure Agreement is signed and added as an exhibit to the agreement in addition to the language found in this section.

I will not, directly or indirectly, use, divulge, or disclose in any manner any information or trade secret(s) disclosed to me or obtained by me or learned by me as result of my participation in the Series, including, without limitation, any and all information concerning or relating to the Series, the participants, the events contained in the Series, the outcome of the Series, the contents of this Agreement, the contents of any document I may sign, have signed, and/or may have received from the Producer and/or Network at any time (collectively, "Confidential Information"), for a period from the date of this Agreement until one (1) year from the initial broadcast of the last episode of the Series in which I participate and/or appear.

> Often the term is three (3) years after the initial broadcast of the last episode of the Series. The participant agrees that these terms mean that it is the last episode of the Series as a whole, as distinct from the episode cycle in which the participant may participate and appear.

The obligations set forth in this Section shall remain in full force and effect whether or not I am selected to participate in the Series, shall continue during and after my participation in the Series, and shall continue regardless of whether an episode of the Series has been broadcast which may include some or all of the Confidential Information.

I acknowledge and agree that violation by me of the terms of this section would cause Producer and the Network irreparable injury and damage that cannot be reasonably or adequately compensated by damages in an action at law, and therefore, I hereby expressly agree that Producer and Network shall be entitled to injunctive and other equitable relief. I also acknowledge and agree that in the event of violation by me of the terms of this Section shall cause Producer and Network substantial and irreparable damages including, but not limited to the following: affecting the Series participants, eliminating tension, surprise, and the outcome of the Series, adversely affecting the ratings of the Series, placing Producer and/or the Network in breach of third party agreements, and given that the extent or amount of such damages would be impractical, difficult, or impossible to calculate or ascertain with certainty or specificity, the parties agree that a reasonable estimate of the damages is in excess of Five Million Dollars ($5,000,000). Accordingly, I agree to pay Producer and/or Network an amount equal to Five Million Dollars ($5,000,000), plus reasonable attorneys' fees, as liquidated damages, and not as a penalty, but rather representing the reasonable endeavor by Producer, Network and me to ascertain the reasonable compensation for the harm which will be incurred by Producer and/or Network as a result of the disclosure.

Participants agree to pay millions of dollars if they reveal confidential information about the show. It has not been reported that any participant has actually paid millions of dollars in accordance with these terms, but there have been reported situations where networks and production companies have exercised their rights. For example, producers of *The Bachelor* filed a lawsuit against an individual who solicited participants on the show for confidential information. The lawsuit reportedly ended in a settlement wherein the individual agreed to stop seeking or releasing such information. Production companies of the show *Survivor* also pursued action against leaks of confidential information about their show. An individual named Jim Early reportedly named one of the *Survivor* contestants, Russell Hantz, as the person providing him the confidential information. It has been reported that production companies for the show *Kitchen Nightmares* exercised its rights found in this paragraph to stop a press conference by the owners of the restaurant "Amy's Baking Company," who were reportedly not happy with their portrayal on the show and sought the opportunity to discuss their experiences on the show.

The statement of "$5,000,000" as liquidated damages may not be upheld in court as a valid amount, because the law requires liquidated damages not be a "penalty" but in fact be a reasonable estimation of the damages to be sustained. Nevertheless, even if the $5,000,000 was held to be invalid, the production companies would get the opportunity to prove what actual damages were suffered by the breach of confidentiality clause. Further, before the filing of any lawsuit, the possibility of paying millions of dollars is a deterrent to individuals who may contemplate revealing such information.

I understand that in the event of a disclosure in violation of this Section I shall be immediately disqualified from continuing any participation in the Series.

It has also been reported that production companies for *The Real Housewives of New Jersey* and *America's Next Top Model* exercised their rights to eliminate participants from their shows, including the reported elimination of the winner of a season of *America's Next Top Model* who was reportedly accused of tweeting that she won the show before the airing of the final episode.

If a judgment is entered against me, Producer and/or Network may take any and all steps necessary to enforce such judgment including, but not limited to, the following: (a) garnishing my wages and/or placing a lien on any property I own (real, tangible, intangible, or otherwise); (b) recovery or disgorgement of monies and/or other consideration I receive in connection with the disclosure; (c) return or recovery of the value of any prize received or to be received in connection with the Series.

A party that wins a claim of breach of confidentiality also has these other remedies of taking money from the losing party's future wages, a return of any prize money, or other money or goods received or to be received.

UNIONS/GUILDS

See Chapter 2.

ARBITRATION

See Chapter 2.

I HAVE BEEN GIVEN AMPLE OPPORTUNITY TO READ, AND I HAVE CAREFULLY READ, THIS ENTIRE AGREEMENT. I REPRESENT AND WARRANT THAT I HAVE THE FULL RIGHT, POWER, AND AUTHORITY TO GRANT THE RIGHTS GRANTED IN THIS AGREEMENT. I CERTIFY THAT I HAVE MADE SUCH AN INVESTIGATION OF THE FACTS PERTINENT TO THIS AGREEMENT AND OF ALL THE MATTERS PERTAINING THERETO AS I HAVE DEEMED NECESSARY, THAT I FULLY UNDERSTAND THE CONTENTS OF THIS AGREEMENT, THAT I AM OF SOUND MIND, AND THAT I INTEND TO BE LEGALLY BOUND BY THIS AGREEMENT. I AM AWARE THAT THIS AGREEMENT IS, AMONG OTHER THINGS, A RELEASE OF LIABILITY FOR FUTURE INJURIES AND A

CONTRACT BETWEEN MYSELF AND PRODUCER AND/ OR ITS AFFILIATED ORGANIZATIONS, AND THAT I AM SIGNING THIS AGREEMENT OF MY OWN FREE WILL. ALL STATEMENTS MADE BY ME IN THIS AGREEMENT ARE TRUE. THE NAME GIVEN BELOW IS MY LEGAL NAME. ANY OTHER NAME(S) OR ALIAS (ES) USED BY ME WITHIN THE PAST FIVE YEARS ARE ALSO NOTED BELOW.

6

On-Air Talent Agreement Between a Production Company and "Talent"

"UNTITLED REALITY SHOW" ON-CAMERA TALENT AGREEMENT FOR FEATURED CAST

Congratulations! A network wants to make a pilot/presentation based on your pitch for a reality television series or the network has ordered your concept straight to series. Once the network has approved the on-camera talent, the producer and the talent will negotiate the terms of the talent's participation on the show. The network production services agreement ("PSA") will provide the parameters of this negotiation.

Although the producer negotiates the deal directly with the talent, in reality it is governed by and done for the benefit of the network. In fact, the PSA will usually condition the network's obligations on its receipt of talent agreements that are compliant with the network guidelines. The fee that the on-camera talent will be paid, the number of options for future cycles, exclusivity, confidentiality, and all other terms in the agreement are dictated by the network. Any deviation from the network's minimum deal requirements must be pre-approved by the network in each instance. If the producer has an attachment agreement in place with the on-camera talent where the majority of the terms have already been negotiated, the network may only require a simple amendment and attachment of its standard terms and conditions in order to make the agreement compliant with network guidelines. Other networks will require the talent to sign a new agreement based on the network-approved form. The talent will not be permitted to appear on camera, including in a casting tape or non-airable presentation, unless the producer and the network have a signed talent agreement in place. To effectuate this, and to handle all other production legal for the project, the network expects the producer to retain an experienced unscripted television production attorney to represent the producer's and the network's interest throughout the production and exploitation of the project.

If the on-camera talent is an unpaid participant who will be regularly featured on the program, a paid participant who will not be regularly featured on the program, or if the participant only appears incidentally on the show, the talent will be provided with an appearance release, which is generally non-negotiable. This chapter does not address these types of agreements.

This chapter features a typical on-camera talent agreement for featured or celebrity talent.

This shall serve to confirm the agreement (the "Agreement") dated as of _____, between _____, Inc. ("Producer") and _____ ("Artist"), in connection with Artist's possible on-camera services on the television series currently entitled _____ ("Series"), currently intended to be initially broadcast on the _____ Network ("Network").

The producer is the person or production company who created, developed, and set the project up with the network for production and exploitation. The producer serves as the production entity for the series. The producer will provide all personnel, materials, and other elements for the series that are not provided by the network, which includes the services of the on-camera talent.

The artist is the on-camera talent, as approved by the network, whom the producer and network expect will appear on multiple cycles of the show (an agreement for an incidental appearance, an unpaid appearance, an appearance by an unknown participant, etc. will not be negotiable unless there is a special circumstance).

The network is the company that has ordered the presentation, pilot, and/or series into production and has engaged the producer to provide production services for the series. In effect, the producer is negotiating the on-camera agreement with the talent for the benefit of the network.

The project is the title of the television series. If the talent is the star of the show, he or she may request approval or meaningful consultation with respect to the title. Unless the talent is a major celebrity, the network will never permit this as a contractual obligation; however, the producer may agree, non-contractually, to meaningfully consult with the talent on the title of the series.

The producer will want the talent excited to be a part of the show—if the talent hates the title, it could start the relationship on the wrong foot.

1. Conditions Precedent: The obligations of Producer under this Agreement are subject to and conditioned upon (a) Artist verifying and delivering to Producer an INS Form I-9 (Employment Eligibility Verification) completed to Producer's satisfaction together with original documents establishing Artist's employment eligibility; and (b) Artist's execution and delivery of this Agreement to Producer.

The agreement will always be structured so that the producer (and the network) will not have any obligation to the talent until certain conditions are met. It may be as simple as conditions that the artist can satisfy, such as completing all employment eligibility forms (e.g., payroll documents, tax and immigration forms, documentation required for statutory record-keeping and identification verification, etc.) and signing the talent agreement. In some instances, however, the producer may include conditions precedent that are not in the talent's absolute control, such as:

(1) The obligations of Producer under this Agreement are subject to and conditioned upon receipt by Producer of signed talent agreements by all of the principal on-camera talent.

(2) The obligations of Producer under this Agreement are subject to and conditioned upon receipt of a signed production services agreement between Network and Producer.

(3) The obligations of Producer under this Agreement are subject to and conditioned upon Network approval of the budget for the Series.

(4) The obligations of Producer under this Agreement are subject to and conditioned upon Network approval of the production schedule for the Series.

(5) The obligations of Producer under this Agreement are subject to and conditioned upon Producer and Network review and approval of a customary background check, psychological evaluation, and/or medical examination of Artist.

(6) The obligations of Producer under this Agreement are subject to and conditioned upon Network approval of the chain-of-title for the Series and the underlying concept.

(7) The obligations of Producer under this Agreement are subject to and conditioned upon Network receipt of a signed agreement between the Producer and any other rights holder.

Even if the agreement is fully executed (i.e., signed by the talent and the producer), if there is a condition precedent that has not been completed, the producer and the network have no obligation to the talent (including no obligation to use the talent's services). The talent representative should request that each condition precedent be deleted, waived, or acknowledged satisfied, and at the very least should request continuing updates on the status of each condition.

2. Series Services:

(a) <u>First Series Year</u>: Producer shall have the exclusive, irrevocable option ("First Series Option") to engage Artist's on–camera services for the first production year of the Series ("First Series Year"). The First Series Option is exercisable by written notice to Artist no later than _____. If Producer exercises the First Series Option, Artist's services in connection with principal photography of the First Series Year will commence on or about a date to be designated by Producer, and Artist shall render such reasonable pre-production services (such as wardrobe fittings, rehearsals, meeting with prospective on-camera judges and other on-camera talent) as Producer may require prior to such date. Provided that Artist is not in uncured material breach or default hereof (which has not been cured subject to the terms of Paragraph 22 below), then, as full compensation for such services and all rights contained therein, Artist shall be entitled to receive a fee of Ten Thousand Dollars ($10,000) per one (1) hour episode or Twenty Thousand Dollars ($20,000) per two (2) hour episode ("Episodic Fee"), with pro rata increases for episodes that are more than fifteen (15) minutes longer than one (1) hour or two (2) hours, as applicable. If Producer exercises the First Series Option, Artist shall be guaranteed compensation on a pay-or-play basis (subject to events of default, disability, and force majeure) for a minimum of thirteen (13) hours for the First Series Year. The Episodic Fee shall be payable on Producer's regularly scheduled payday the week following the completion of principal photography of the applicable episode. The First Series Year may include more than one (1) production cycle, and Producer may, in its sole discretion, engage Artist to render services in any such production cycle beyond the initial production cycle (provided Artist was engaged for the immediately preceding production cycle) for the same Episodic Fee set forth above in this Paragraph. Each episode of the Series, regardless of length, for which Artist is engaged pursuant to this Agreement, is sometimes referred to as an "Episode."

Once the producer and the network elect to engage the talent, the producer will exercise the talent's option to engage the talent's on-camera services in connection with the first series year of the program. Once exercised, the talent will be committed to rendering on-camera services and any other services that the producer and/or network require in accordance with the terms of this agreement.

This option structure benefits the producer and the network by allowing time for the network to decide if it will order an initial production cycle and to decide if the talent is the best fit for the series. The parties may agree to a certain date by which the talent's first series option must be exercised, or the option exercise may be based on some triggering date (e.g., three months after final delivery of the pilot). The talent may also require that the exercise of his or her option be tied to that of any other on-camera talent (i.e., if you exercise one person's on-camera services, you must simultaneously exercise the services of all on-camera talent).

Regardless of how it is structured, the talent will want the option exercise period to be as short as possible. It is unlikely that the talent will be rendering services for the producer or network during this time (or permitted to render services for others), and the talent is not typically paid for this holding period. The shorter the option exercise period, the less time the talent is held off of the market. A-level celebrity talent, however, can request protection in a number of ways:

(1) The talent can refuse to agree to an option period. In this regard, the producer and network are forced to engage the talent upon signature of the talent agreement, or risk that another producer and/or network will engage the talent's services.

(2) The talent may require a holding fee. If the talent is essential to a network order and the success of the series, the talent representative will request payment in exchange for the talent holding him- or herself off of the market. The talent representative will further request that the fee is not recoupable (i.e., will not have to paid back to the producer). If the fee is recoupable, the holding fee serves as a guarantee against subsequent participation in the program.

(3) The talent may insist on a non-order fee. If the producer does not receive an order for the first series year, the producer agrees to pay artist a one-time fee.

Once the producer exercises the option for the talent's on-camera services, the producer will set a start date. Depending on the amount of negotiating power of the on-camera talent, his or her representative may request a start date that is mutually agreed to by the parties. If the talent has another career (e.g., the talent is a professional athlete under contract with a team), the talent might further request good-faith, meaningful consultation with regard to the production schedule. The network will be hesitant to contractually agree to a production schedule that is subject to the availability of the on-camera talent, because this could be used down the line to refuse to render *any* on-camera services. If the network and producer agree, however, the talent should be required to make him- or herself available for a minimum number of pre-production and shooting days and further clarify that, once set, the talent will not be able to alter the production schedule unless a bona fide, unforeseeable professional obligation arises.

The network will determine how a "series year" is defined. A series year may equal one series cycle or one calendar year. It is to the producer and network's benefit to define a series year as 365 days, whereby they may be able to produce two or three cycles in one calendar year without exercising an additional series option for the talent's services. This is rarely, if ever, negotiable by the talent, as this is usually a network policy.

Compensation

The talent agreement will also confirm the fee that the talent will be paid for each episode (the "episodic fee"). The episodic fee may have been agreed to in a talent attachment agreement, or it may be discussed for the first time in this agreement. The amount paid per episode will vary based on the level of interest the project has garnered from competing networks, the talent's celebrity status, the fan-base of the talent, the talent's associates (e.g., if the talent's spouse is a celebrity who is likely to appear on the program, the talent may be able to negotiate for a higher episodic fee), the amount that the talent has been paid in the past for similar services (i.e., the talent's precedent), the budget of each episode of the program, and any other factor that the parties find relevant in negotiating the per-episode fee.

Once the talent's services are engaged (i.e., the option is exercised), the talent will want to ensure that his or her services are "pay-or-play" and the talent is guaranteed to appear in "all shows produced" (i.e., the talent will be paid for each episode of the program produced during the first series cycle, regardless of whether the talent is required to render on-camera services). The producer will push back on both points. The producer will not want to be obligated to pay the talent for services that he or she does not actually render and will want the freedom to replace the talent at its option, even mid-cycle if appropriate. If the talent is a celebrity, host, or judge, their representative should do everything possible to secure "pay-or-play" language and a guarantee of some or all shows produced. This is the only way to secure the talent's continued involvement in the series and to ensure that the talent is paid for all of the services he or she renders.

(b) Second and Subsequent Series Years. Producer shall also have six (6) consecutive, dependent, exclusive, and irrevocable options (each a "Subsequent Series Year Option"; together with the First Series Option, each a "Series Option") to engage Artist's on-camera services pursuant to the next six (6) production years of the Series (each a "Subsequent Series Year"; the First Series Year and any Subsequent Series Year for which Producer exercises an option hereunder shall collectively be referred to herein as a "Series Year"). Artist's Episodic Fee for each Subsequent Series Year for which Producer exercises its Subsequent Series Year Option, if any, shall increase by Two Thousand Five Hundred Dollars ($2,500) per hour of programming on an annual basis (i.e. Twelve Thousand Five Hundred Dollars ($12,500) per hour of programming for the second Series Year, Fifteen Thousand Dollars ($15,000) per hour of programming for the third Series Year, Seventeen Thousand Five Hundred Dollars ($17,500) per hour of programming for the fourth Series Year, Twenty Thousand Dollars ($20,000) per hour of programming for the fifth Series Year, Twenty-Two Thousand Five Hundred Dollars ($22,500) per hour of programming for the sixth Series Year, and Twenty-Five Thousand Dollars ($25,000) per hour of programming for the seventh Series Year), with pro rata increases for episodes that are more than fifteen (15) minutes longer than one (1) or two (2) hours. For each Series Year for which Producer exercises its Subsequent Series Year Option, Artist shall be guaranteed compensation on a pay-or-play basis (subject to events of default, disability, and force majeure) for all episodes for the applicable production cycle(s) for which Artist is engaged in the applicable Series Year with a minimum of thirteen (13) hours of programming for the applicable Series Year. The Episodic Fee shall be payable on Producer's regularly scheduled payday the week following the completion of principal photography of the applicable episode for which Artist renders and completes all required services. Any Subsequent Series Year may include more than one (1) production cycle, and Producer may, in its sole discretion, engage Artist to render services in any such production cycle beyond the initial production cycle of such Subsequent Series Year (provided Artist was engaged for the immediately preceding production cycle) for the same Episodic Fee. Producer may exercise each Subsequent Series Year Option (if at all) by written notice to Artist within nine and one-half (9 ½) months after final delivery to Network of the last episode produced for the immediately preceding Series Year.

The producer will always require options to exercise the talent's on-camera services for subsequent cycles of the series. As a rule, the network will require that the producer obtain the same number of options to engage the talent's on-camera services as the network has to engage the producer's production services. In most instances, the number of options is not negotiable by the talent unless a limit is agreed to from the outset. Of course, the network/producer will always want the most options possible and the talent will want the fewest number that the network/producer will agree to. Once the options expire, the talent is free to negotiate for a better deal with the producer or to choose to no longer be involved with the series. When a show is successful, this puts the producer in a very difficult position. The parties typically agree to 4–6 additional options for subsequent series cycles.

The talent and his or her representative should note that if California law governs the talent agreement, the duration of any personal services contract is limited to seven years (California Labor Code §2855). Even if the producer still has options to engage the service of the talent, once seven years have passed, the talent is no longer obligated to render services for the producer.

Once the option for a subsequent series year is exercised, the fee that the talent is paid per episode will increase. The parties may negotiate a specific dollar increase for each series year, or they may agree to increase the episodic fee by 4–5% for each additional cycle. Regardless of the episodic increase the parties agree to in the talent agreement, the talent representative is free to approach the producer and request more money upon the exercise of the option. If the series is a success, the producer and network will likely agree to a higher episodic fee (or some other additional compensation) in order to keep the talent excited to be a part of the project.

3. Exclusivity:

(a) Except as otherwise specifically provided below, Artist shall be exclusive to Producer as on-camera talent in all television programming and in all substantially similar productions in any media (Producer shall use reasonable good faith efforts to obtain Network's approval for Artist to appear in theatrical motion pictures and scripted programming provided Artist's services hereunder remain in first position) and in the following "Ancillary Products": products/merchandise (including, but not limited to, DVDs, books, clubs, etc.), ancillary applications (including, without limitation, online clubs and mobile applications), and services (including, without limitation, cruises, expos, resorts), from the date of this agreement through the end of the last broadcast year for which Producer has exercised its applicable Series Option (provided Producer has no further unexpired Series Option remaining); provided, however, that Artist may appear in Ancillary Products that do not prevent Artist from appearing in Series-branded Ancillary Products, it being understood that such Ancillary Products in which Artist may appear may be in the same product categories (e.g., DVDs, books, clubs, etc.) as Series-branded Ancillary Products, as long as Artist also appears and participates in Series-branded Ancillary Products to the extent required by Producer. All services are first priority to Producer and rendered on a full-time, in person, no material interference basis. Notwithstanding anything stated in this Agreement, Artist's permitted services to third parties shall not: (i) be rendered during production periods; (ii) interfere with Artist's first priority obligations to Studio; (iii) denigrate the Series, Network, or other license(s); or (iv) portray or parody Artist's role or the Series. For purposes of clarity and without limiting the foregoing, in no event shall Artist grant any third party the right to use Artist's name, voice, or other likeness in or in connection with any exploitation based on, or related to or trading off of, the Series or Artist's role therein.

(b) Artist shall not appear in any commercials or endorsements without Producer's and Network's prior written approval, not to be unreasonably withheld. Notwithstanding the foregoing, subject to the conditions set forth in this paragraph, Artist may render services on one (1) national commercial campaign during each year hereunder, subject to the Network's reasonable approval (such approval not to be unreasonably withheld), provided that commercials for and endorsements of Artist's own products (as opposed to those promoting or endorsing a third-party sponsor) shall not be subject to the foregoing approval rights or one campaign per year limitation; provided that [i] if the Series involves product integration, then notwithstanding the foregoing, Artist may not render services on any endorsement for any product which is competitive with the product(s) of any sponsors that are integrated into the Series (promptly following Artist's written request, Producer shall furnish Artist a list of any such then-current sponsors), and [ii] at no time in the Series Term may Artist appear in a new commercial campaign while an old campaign in which Artist appears is still being broadcast. Any such request may be disapproved only for the following reasons: (1) the commercial engagement conflicts with a major sponsor or advertiser; (2) the commercial engagement is in connection with alcohol, tobacco, or firearms; (3) the commercial engagement is an in-character portrayal or trades off the character portrayed (but Producer acknowledges that Artist shall be appearing as herself/himself on the Series, and accordingly any such commercial engagement in which Artist appears as herself/himself shall not be deemed a breach hereof so long as Artist does not specifically refer to Artist's participation in the Series without Producer's or Network's prior written consent); or (4) the content of the specific commercial engagement may be detrimental to the Series, Producer, or Network, or otherwise denigrates or reflects negatively on such. In addition, notwithstanding the foregoing, subject to the conditions set forth in this paragraph, Artist shall have the right to render unidentifiable, off-screen voiceover services in an unlimited number of commercials and public service announcements (and, for the avoidance of doubt, theatrical motion pictures, movies-for-television, radio programs, and other projects not prohibited by Artist's television and episodic digital media exclusivity as set forth above) and Artist shall have the right to render services in an unlimited number of foreign commercials (solely if the agreement for Artist's services in such foreign commercials provides that such commercials may not be broadcast in the United States); provided that the aforementioned services are in second position to and do not materially interfere with Artist's obligations to Producer hereunder.

Any permitted services of Artist for others are in second position and subject to Artist's obligation to render services hereunder, and no such permitted services shall materially interfere with Artist's services hereunder.

When the on-camera talent is a celebrity or has more leverage than an unknown participant, the exclusivity provision is often one of the most significant components of the agreement. Even if a talent attachment agreement is in place that defines the parameters of the talent's exclusivity, it will likely be subject to any additional exclusivity required by the applicable network once the project is "set up." The network is always hesitant to agree to anything other than absolute exclusivity and will not want the talent to appear in or provide any other services whatsoever for any other television, digital, or online network.

As a rule, the bigger the celebrity, the more permissive the exclusivity provision will be. If the talent is a noted actor in scripted television and film, it will be nearly impossible to close a deal that does not permit the talent to continue to render those services. If the talent is a well-known host, he or she may ask to be exclusive to the producer during the broadcast of the initial run of the series only. If the talent is a judge who was chosen for his or her celebrity and expertise, they may request freedom to participate in any other program so long as it is not scheduled to be exhibited at the same time as any regularly scheduled exhibition of the series. The exclusivity provision should always be tailored to the talent in a manner that benefits both parties. When you turn on the television, it is common to see celebrities rendering services for more than one television show that is in its initial broadcast. For example, Ryan Seacrest has at one point or another rendered services simultaneously for shows broadcast on various networks, including on-camera services for *American Idol* (Fox) and *E! News* (E!) while producing numerous other scripted and unscripted television shows including *Shahs of Sunset* (Bravo), *Mixology* (ABC), and *The Million Second Quiz* (NBC). In most instances, it will benefit the series if the talent is successful in other aspects of his or her career.

Even if the producer is flexible with the parameters of the talent's exclusivity, the producer will almost certainly require that the talent's services be rendered for the producer on a first priority, full-time, in-person, no material interference basis during all periods of production. The producer will only agree to be in second position as it relates to pre-existing commitments or if the talent is a celebrity who will only agree to material, no-interference exclusivity so that he or she can continue to render services in scripted television and film.

Ancillary Use:

An ancillary use is any distribution or exploitation of the series or any series elements other than on the network or on an affiliated distribution service, which may include merchandising, publishing, soundtracks, theme parks, promotional or commercial tie-ins, or any other mechanism used to promote the series off of the network. During production periods, these services will always be rendered on a first priority basis; at all other times, the services are typically subject to the talent's availability (see also section 10 below relating to guaranteed ancillary services). It will be of particular importance to the producer and network that the talent does not permit a third party to use the talent's name or likeness in a manner that trades off of the series or the talent's role in the series (i.e., the talent is not permitted to engage in creating his or her own ancillary products or services). Where it is appropriate, pursuant to the exclusivity provision contained in the talent agreement, for the talent to render services for parties other than the producer and/or network, it is also of particular importance that the talent does not portray or parody the talent's role on the series nor do anything that would cast the series, or the artist's involvement, in a negative light.

Commercials and Endorsements

It will also be particularly important to the network that the talent agrees that he or she will not appear in or authorize the use of his or her name or likeness in commercials or pursuant to endorsement agreements without first obtaining the network's approval. With this in mind, the network will never permit the talent to engage in these services on behalf of products or services that are competitive to the network or any of its sponsors or advertisers unless the commitment pre-exists this agreement. The network and producer will want to further limit the talent's ability to enter into any agreement that would restrict the network's and/or producer's right to use the talent's name, voice, and likeness for the purposes agreed to in the talent agreement.

The network and producer may, however, allow the talent to render certain services without seeking network permission, so long as the services are rendered in second position to the series and do not materially interfere with any of the artist's obligations to the series. Examples of outside services that may be automatically permitted include:

- Voice-over services in commercials; provided that neither Artist nor the Series is identifiable in the commercial. Further, the commercial should not promote a product or service that is competitive to a production or service of the network or a network sponsor or advertiser.

- Public service announcements.

- Foreign commercials (i.e., commercials that will not be broadcast in the United States).

If the network pre-approves certain commercial or endorsement services, the permitted services (and the parameters of the services) will always be explicitly defined in the talent agreement.

4. <u>No Additional Compensation</u>: The compensation payable to Artist is all-inclusive for all of Artist's services on the Series, including, without limitation, pre-production, production, and post-production services, promotional services, and any other services described herein for which additional payment is not specified. No increased or additional compensation shall be payable by reason of Artist's rendition of services at night, on Saturdays, Sundays, or holidays, for travel time, or after the expiration of any particular number of hours in

any one day. The compensation set forth in this Agreement for Artist's services shall constitute payment for all runs and all other exploitation of the Series episodes on the Network and in any and all other media now known or hereafter devised, through the universe in perpetuity. Artist hereby consents to the exhibition and exploitation of the Series and/or strips or clips therefrom in all media including, without limitation, supplemental markets and interactive electronic media in perpetuity throughout the universe, for no additional compensation. Without limiting the foregoing, Artist's services hereunder shall include services in connection with (a) the production of new and/or enhanced material related to the Series intended for exhibition in short segments (e.g., approximate run times of no more than 15 minutes) (including, but not limited to, material specifically produced for intended initial exploitation via broadband, internet, any portable audio and/or video device [e.g., iPod, cellular phone, mp3 player], DVD, or any other present or future non-television distribution media—e.g., webisodes, mobisodes, DVD extras, etc.) ("Enhanced Material"); and (b) participating in Series-related tradeouts and Series-related product integrations with respect to in-program content (including, without limitation, verbally mentioning, referring to, touching, and/or interacting with products, but not as a direct or personal endorsement, subject to paragraph 6 below).

In addition to on-camera services required during production of the series (e.g., on-camera shoot days, on-camera introductions, narration, voiceover services, pick-ups, etc.), the talent will be required to render additional services. Customary additional services may include:

- Pre-production services, e.g., wardrobe fittings, makeup tests, attending casting sessions, meeting with prospective on-camera judges and other on-camera talent, rehearsals, filmed interviews, publicity and production stills, meetings relating to the story arc of the season, music or other production matters, and any other pre-production service reasonably requested by the producer and/or network. Regardless of the negotiating power of the talent, the talent representative should ensure that these services are subject to the talent's prior professional commitments.

- Post production services, e.g., post-synchronization, voice-overs, looping/ADR (Automatic Dialog Replacement), dubbing, retakes, or any additional services required by the producer to complete each series episode of the applicable cycle.

- Participating in the filming of lead-ins, leadouts, on-camera introductions, wraparounds, on-camera commentary and interviews, voiceover materials, mini-episodes, so-called "after shows," behind-the-scenes and "making-of" content, and other extended programming content.

- Promotional services, which may include appearances at press and media events (e.g., Television Critics Association (TCA) Press Tour), print, radio and television interviews (e.g. news shows, morning shows, talk shows), satellite media tours, awards shows (see also section 5 below relating to promotion and publicity services).

- Still photography sessions, attending promotional screenings, personal appearances.

- Participation in services that do not require the talent to be present to be in-person, namely online promotional activities (e.g., blogs, webisodes, social media, user-generated or user-uploaded content-based sites, participation in online chat sessions, responding to emails, etc.).

- Product integrations, product demonstrations, sponsored promotional announcements or interstitials, and/or other similar sponsor-related refer-ences, information, or activities. This may include naming, using, describing, wearing, demonstrating, and/or otherwise referencing or interacting with sponsor products, services, and brands.

- Participation in production of new and/or enhanced material related to the Series (e.g., DVD extras, webisodes, internet shorts, bonus material for down-load, blogs, video diaries, etc.)

The talent's episodic compensation will be inclusive of payment for these additional services unless indicated otherwise in the agreement (see also section 10 below relating to guaranteed ancillary services).

As noted in previous chapters, most unscripted talent agreements are not governed by the guild that oversees the working conditions of on-camera talent—SAG-AFTRA.

Without protection from the guild, the on-camera talent is not guaranteed minimum compensation, additional payment for overtime work, etc. A celebrity may be able to place limits on the amount of hours worked per day; however, the producer will not likely agree to this, or any other additional protections.

5. <u>Promotion</u>. Artist shall render all services reasonably required by Producer and the Network in connection with promotion, advertising, and marketing of the Series. Subject to Artist's professional availability if not during principal photography periods, Artist will render promotional and publicity services in connection with the Series as required by Producer and/or Network (and such services shall be rendered by Artist on a first priority basis once dates are scheduled), including, without limitation, attending a reasonable and customary number of publicity and promotion activities (including, without limitation, major media events, network affiliate functions, and Producer's events in connection with the Series), and making a reasonable number of tours (including, without limitation, tours that involve promoting the Series and/or Series-related merchandising, publishing, or other ancillary exploitation, promotional tours which may include promoting Series-related merchandise and Series-related ancillaries) and public appearances (including, without limitation, media appearances on news, talk, and late-night programming in any and all media) for no additional compensation. It is of the essence to this Agreement that Artist makes himself/herself available to appear and participate in the following publicity activities as required by Network and/or Producer: (a) the "up front" presentations; (b) at least one photography session, upon two weeks' notice to Artist, either before, during, or after production; (c) the Television Critics Association (TCA) press tours; (d) Series-related promotional appearances on news and talk shows; and (e) Series-related tours. In addition, Artist will be available, subject to Artist's prior professional commitments during non-production

periods, to appear and participate, if so requested by the Network and/ or Producer, in the following for no additional compensation. (i) a reasonable and customary number of photography sessions conducted by Network, Producer, or Network's or Producer's photographers at the production site, on location, or in the gallery; (ii) a reasonable and customary number of appearances in promotional announcements in which Network, Producer, and/or any sponsors, product integration partners, and tradeout partners may desire to produce; (iii) a minimum of three half-day telephone interviews with television writers arranged by Network; (iv) a reasonable and customary number of major media events, if any; (v) any pre-launch shows that take place at the beginning of each broadcast season to promote the Network's entire lineup (including, without limitation, custom promotions for affiliates); and (vi) the press tour at the start of each broadcast season and other press interviews.

The producer will contractually require the talent to render a variety of publicity services to allow the producer to fully promote the series. Any and all promotional services fall under the category of "additional services," and the talent will not receive any further compensation or remuneration in consideration for his or her participation in the required publicity services. If the promotion, advertising, and marketing services are rendered during principal photography, the talent will be required to appear whenever the producer requires. If the additional promotional services occur outside of principal photography, then the services will typically be subject to the talent's professional availability so long as the talent uses reasonable good faith efforts to be available.

Because what constitutes a "reasonable" amount of services can be argued by the talent once the services are requested (for example, the talent may render a few promotional services, deem those services a reasonable amount, and refuse to render any additional services), networks often require that the producer specifically list the promotional services that the talent is expected to render in the talent agreement. The talent must participate in and/or attend all of the promotional events listed in the talent agreement or else risk being in breach. The representative of a celebrity may be able to negotiate for fewer services (for example, one half-day of interviews as opposed to three half-days);

however, even that will be difficult. The producer will argue that the requirements are not onerous as all of the services will be subject to the talent's professional availability. Moreover, although a laundry list of promotional services are detailed in the talent agreement, the producer and/or network may not require the talent to render all (or any) of the services listed.

If the talent is a celebrity, the producer may agree to consult meaningfully with the talent regarding any promotional services that the talent is expected to render. The talent's representative should ensure that the talent is not required to participate in any promotion or advertisement that the talent finds offensive. If the producer does agree to this limitation, however, the producer should require that the talent will render other comparable services if the talent refuses any particular request. For example, if the talent does not want to be interviewed by a particular host or on a particular program, the talent will not be required to do so as long as they agree to a similar interview elsewhere.

6. <u>In-Show Integrations</u>: Artist acknowledges and agrees that the Series may frequently feature advertiser sponsored in-show product integrations, and Artist acknowledges and agrees that Producer and/or Network have the right to use Artist's services, and Artist's name, voice, and/or likeness, and to reasonably require Artist's cooperation in connection with such integrations, provided that Artist will not be required to, and Artist's name, voice, and/or likeness will not be used to, directly and personally endorse any such product or service without Artist's prior consent. For the avoidance of doubt, requiring Artist to say the name of and/or describe the features of a product or service (including any model name, brand name, or sub-brand name), and/or to touch, hold, or otherwise interact with a particular product or service, shall not alone be deemed to constitute a direct personal endorsement. Examples of direct personal endorsements are: "I use this product" or "I like this product." Producer shall control all product integration agreements and all tradeout agreements in connection with the Series, and Artist shall not have the right to negotiate or enter into product integration agreements or tradeout agreements in connection with the Series.

An unscripted television series will often feature advertiser sponsored in-show product integrations. The producer will require the talent to participate in series-related tradeouts and series-related product integrations with respect to in-program content. The talent will need to acknowledge that the network has the right to use the talent's name and likeness in connection with such integrations.

This right is essential for the network; however, the talent can limit this right by asking the network to agree that the talent's name, voice, and/or likeness will not be used to directly and personally endorse any product or service without the talent's consent (e.g., the talent will not be forced to say "I use this product" unless the talent has agreed). If the talent warrants a further accommodation, the producer may agree that the talent will not be represented as using, consuming, or endorsing any product, commodity, or service (other than the series itself) without the talent's prior consent.

7. <u>Name, Likeness, Etc</u>.: Artist grants to Producer and Network and their respective licensees (for no additional compensation) the right to use Artist's name, photo, voice, approved (in accordance with the provisions set forth below) biography, and approved (in accordance with the provisions set forth below) likeness in and in connection with the Series, in advertising and promotions for the Series (including, without limitation, advertising and/or promotions including Series sponsors, advertisers, product integration partners, and tradeout partners), and to advertise or publicize Network, the Series, and/or any episode of the Series (including, without limitation, the ancillary exploitation thereof), in any manner or media worldwide in perpetuity, now known or hereafter devised (including, without limitation, via the Internet, on subscription-based websites, mobile devices including, but not limited to, ringtones, screen images, pictures, graphics, text, games, animations, video, software applications, SMS, EMS, or MMS alerts and/or applications, voice recorded greetings or messages, individually or in a collection or compilation of any of these materials), and in Series-related commercial tie-ins in any and all media (including, without limitation, in print, on television, online, and in-store), including, without

limitation, for any sponsor for the Series or any product integration/ tradeout partner for the Series provided that it does not constitute a product and direct endorsement. Artist shall work with Producer and any distributors/networks/licensees, production integration partners, and sponsors of the Series to promote the Series. Upon Producer's request, Artist shall furnish Artist's biography, and Producer shall use only information contained in such biography in connection with the exploitation of Producer's rights hereunder, provided that if such biography is not promptly delivered (i.e., within seventy-two (72) hours) to Producer, Producer shall have the right to use biographical material obtained elsewhere. Artist shall have approval of still photographs and art likenesses of Artist that are issued by or under the direct control of Producer to advertise and promote the Series; provided, however, that Artist shall approve at least fifty percent (50%) of a reasonable number of such photographs submitted to Artist in which Artist appears alone, and provided that Artist shall approve seventy-five percent (75%) of a reasonable number of photographs in which Artist appears with any other person. With respect to Artist's art likeness, if Artist disapproves of the first artwork submitted to Artist, Producer shall be obligated to redraw Artist's likeness not more than two (2) times; if Artist is still not satisfied with the redrawn artwork, Producer shall nevertheless be entitled to use such last-redrawn likeness (or other prior drawn likeness if Artist so notifies Producer within the applicable time period set forth below) for any and all purposes hereunder as it relates to any and all aspects of the Series. Producer agrees to use its good faith efforts to incorporate any changes or revisions to the artwork as proposed by Artist. Artist (or Artist's designee) agrees to approve or disapprove such photographs and/or likenesses within three (3) business days (reducible to one (1) business day in the case of actual production and promotional exigencies upon written notice received by Artist and Artist's representative) from receipt by Artist or Artist's representative after being asked to do so, and Artist shall be deemed to have approved all such photographs and/or likenesses if Artist fails to respond within said period. Artist's approval of any photographs and/or likenesses with respect to the advertising and promotion of the Series as provided herein shall be deemed approval of such photographs and/or likenesses for any other authorized purpose under the Agreement. For the avoidance of doubt, Artist's approval rights pursuant to this paragraph shall apply only to still photographs and art likenesses of Artist that are issued by or under the direct control of Producer, and shall not apply to those issued by or under the control of the Network or any third party, but Producer agrees to notify the Network of Artist's approval rights pursuant to this paragraph, and shall use reasonable good faith efforts to cause the Network to abide by such requirements. At Artist's election, Artist's representative may view and approve or disapprove any such photographs and/or likenesses on Artist's behalf.

Each and every talent representative will ask for name, likeness, and biography approval; however, the network will rarely permit the producer to grant it for talent on an unscripted series. If the producer does grant this approval (usually to a judge, host, or celebrity), then the producer will place parameters around the extent of the talent's approval right.

Generally, the biography must be provided within a certain time period following signature of the agreement or at the producer's request. Once the biography is submitted, the producer agrees to only use facts contained in the biography. The producer, however, almost always retains the right to reformat the biography and use only the facts that the producer chooses.

If the talent receives approval of still images, the producer will either require approval of a reasonable amount of photographs or the talent will be permitted to "kill" a certain number of photos. In most instances, the talent will be required to approve at least 50% of photographs submitted to the talent in which the talent appears alone, and 75% if the talent appears with any other person who also has likeness approval. If the talent does not approve the required percentage of photographs, the producer generally reserves the right to choose additional photos on the talent's behalf in order to meet the approval percentage. Only A-level celebrities will be granted an absolute approval over images used of him or her in connection with an unscripted series.

Occasionally, the producer will use an artistic rendering of an artist instead of a photograph, and the talent will also want the right to approve the artwork before it is used. The producer will either agree to good faith efforts to incorporate any reasonable changes to the artwork or the producer will agree to a certain number of "likeness passes" (e.g., if the talent has two likeness passes, the artist will make changes based on the talent's comments and present the art to the talent for a second review and set of revisions. After the second pass by the artist, the artistic rendering is deemed final).

Once the talent's likeness and/or biography is approved, the producer will have the right to use (and license to others the right to use) the photo and information wherever the producer chooses in connection with the exploitation of the series.

8. Commercials/Promotional Episodes/Other Program Materials: Producer and/or the Network shall have the right to require Artist to render a reasonable amount of services on program commercials, advertising, marketing, and promotional materials, whether on-air or otherwise, of any kind or nature in connection with the exploitation, advertising, or promotion of the Series, for which Artist shall receive no additional compensation. Producer shall also have the right to require Artist to render services in a reasonable number (subject to customary Network requirements) of standard openings, closings, bridges, lead-ins, lead-outs, teasers, promos, bumpers, and trailers (however denom-inated) for no additional compensation provided such services shall be subject to Artist's professional availability if not during principal photography periods of the Series (provided Artist shall use reasonable good faith efforts to be available when reasonably required hereunder).

The producer and network will want the contractual right to require the talent to render on-camera services in connection with any commercial that promotes the series or a spe-cific episode of the series. The producer will also request that the talent render services in connection with advertising series-related merchandise, and that the talent render series-related services for promotional segments and cross-plugs. Each of the forego-ing falls under "additional services" and the talent will not be given any additional compensation to render these services unless agreed to elsewhere in the agreement. Of course, if the services are not rendered during principal photography, the services will be subject to the talent's processional availability, so long as the talent makes good faith efforts to make him or herself available to render the commercial services.

9. <u>Merchandising, Ancillary Exploitation, and Commercial Tie-Ins</u>: Artist grants to Producer the right to use Artist's name, likeness, biography, and voice in connection with Series-related merchandising, Series-related commercial tie-ins, other ancillary exploitation of the Series, and soundtrack album(s), publishing, and/or other phonorecords derived from the soundtrack of the Series. At the request of Producer and/or the Network, Artist may be reasonably required, subject to Artist's professional availability outside of Series production periods, to provide services that do not require Artist to be in-person (whether during or outside Series production periods) for Series-related ancillary exploitation for no additional compensation which may include, without limitation, participating in online chat sessions, writing blog entries (or approving online blog entries written by a ghost writer), writing forewords and/or afterwords for Series-related books, and responding to e-mails (or approving responses to e-mails written by a ghost writer) to questions/comments sent into a subscription-based website. For the purposes of clarity, Producer shall control all Series-related merchandising and all Series-related ancillary exploitation, provided Producer shall not use Artist's name, likeness, biography, or voice in connection with the following items of merchandising, without Artist's prior written consent: Alcohol, tobacco, firearms, pharmaceuticals, undergarments, and personal hygiene products. Artist shall not have the right to create, authorize, license, or otherwise permit Series-related merchandising and/or Series-related ancillary exploitation, or provide services for same, without Producer's prior written approval. Artist shall be entitled to the following royalty for Series-related merchandise featuring

Artist's name, voice, and/or likeness: five percent (5%) of Producer's Net Receipts reducible by other individual entitled to receive a royalty on the same item of merchandising to two and one-half percent (2 ½%) of Producer's Net Receipts. Net Receipts shall be computed in accordance with Producer's customary accounting practices, including deduction of any merchandising royalties payable to third party participants (but not any that reduce Artist's participation below five percent (5%) of Producer's Net Receipts) and deduction of a distribution fee of thirty-five percent (35%) of gross receipts (inclusive of all fees and sub-distribution fees and any costs and expenses (including, without limitation, legal fees).

The producer will require the right to use the talent's name, likeness, biography, and voice in connection with merchandising, commercial tie-ins, and any other ancillary exploitation of the series. The talent will request approval over each and every use of his or her name, likeness, and biography and will want to limit the use to in connection with the exploitation of the series (as opposed to use separate and apart from the series to promote the network and/or producer generally). Unless the talent is a celebrity, the producer will likely refuse to grant such an approval right. If the producer refuses to grant an approval right to the talent, then the talent's representation should ask for "standard exclusions" (e.g., the talent's name and likeness cannot be used in any ancillary products or merchandise that promotes or relates to alcohol, gambling, religious items, tobacco, firearms, weapons, drugs, pornographic material, undergarments, personal hygiene items, etc.). Whatever name, likeness, and image approvals the parties agreed to in section 7 will also apply here (i.e., if the talent has likeness approval, then the producer may only use an approved image on any merchandising or ancillary product).

The representative of a celebrity (or any other talent who has more negotiating power than the average participant) should always ensure that their client receives a royalty for any merchandising use of the talent's name or likeness. The standard merchandising royalty is 5% of net merchandising receipts, reducible to 2½% if the talent appears with other on-camera talent who are also entitled to a royalty. The talent will want to be sure that the net merchandising revenue will be computed and accounted for in accordance with the producer's standard definition and subject to good faith negotiation by the parties once applicable.

If the talent is a celebrity and/or already has personal merchandising products on the market (e.g. a professional athlete), the talent will want to further clarify that he or she will have the right to continue to engage in personal merchandising activities. If the producer agrees, to prevent overlap, the talent's personal merchandising activity should not mention or refer to the series in any way.

10. Ancillary Services Guarantee: For each year (which year shall begin on the earliest of the premiere date of the first episode of such Series year or the first date that such services in connection with ancillary products are provided by Artist at Producer's written request) for which at least one (1) option is exercised, Artist will be guaranteed payment of Two Thousand Seven Hundred Fifty Dollars ($2,750) per full day of in person services for a minimum of fifteen (15) days (i.e., a guaranteed payment of Forty-One Thousand Two Hundred Fifty Dollars ($41,250)) for services in connection with ancillary products such as books, appearances on home-shopping network type programs (e.g., QVC, HSN), products of sponsors, product integration partners, and tradeout partners, merchandising, DVD and home video products, video games (including, without limitation, on-camera, motion capture, and/or voiceover services) and Series-related ancillary applications (including, without limitation, tours before paying audiences, events before paying audiences, mobile applications, Internet applications (e.g., webisodes, weblogs which may be text, audio or audio-visual, interactive media, online clubs, subscription websites, social networking websites or web-pages, etc.), and the marketing and promotion thereof. Producer shall have the option for any number of additional days of such services, beyond the initial fifteen (15) days, at the same rate of Two Thousand Seven Hundred Fifty Dollars ($2,750) per day. No payment for Series promotion which may also involve ancillary products and no payment for ancillary services which are not rendered in person. For the purposes of this Agreement, rendering services "in person" shall be defined

as Artist traveling to a location at Producer's request to render services (e.g., on-camera or in-studio voice-over services for a Series-related DVD or video game, appearance on a home shopping network-type program, etc.), but shall not include services which Artist may render from Artist's residence/business/primary location without traveling (e.g., blogging, participating in a web chat or Skype session, providing voiceover services via an ISDN line, writing selected content for a subscription based website, etc.). Ancillary services shall be scheduled in accordance with Artist's professional availability if not during or consecutive to production periods, provided once scheduled, Artist shall be first priority to Producer on the days scheduled. Unless Artist receives written confirmation from Producer's business and legal affairs department (which may include confirmation via e-mail) that Artist is being paid for one of the above described in person services prior to rendering such services, Artist should not expect any compensation for such services; Producer shall endeavor to give at least seven (7) days prior written notice of such services.

> Most networks do not provide an additional fee for providing ancillary services; however, some networks will provide additional compensation to the talent if he or she provides additional services specifically relating to products of a sponsor/advertiser, co-promotion of the series, merchandising, events in front of paying audiences, personal appearances, publicity tours and the like. If these services are rendered in-person (i.e. he or she travels to a location at the producer's or network's request to render services), and the network confirms that the talent will be paid additional compensation, then the talent will receive the pre-determined fee set forth in the talent agreement or a fee to be negotiated in good faith. The compensation and types of services that the talent may be required to render are typically uniform across the network for all of its talent; therefore, it is almost always non-negotiable. These additional services are always scheduled pursuant to the talent's professional availability if outside of production periods; provided that once the date is set the ancillary services become the talent's first priority.

11. <u>Results and Proceeds/Grant of Rights/Rights</u>: See Chapter 2.

12. <u>Credit</u>: Subject to Network credit policies, and provided Artist is not in material breach or material default hereof (which has not been cured subject to the terms of Paragraph 22 below). Producer shall accord Artist an on-camera credit on each episode of the Series for which Artist renders and completes all required services. The foregoing credit shall be no less favorable with respect to size and style of type as to any other credit accorded to any other on-camera Series regular on the Series. In the event that credit is accorded to any other on-camera Series regular in any paid advertising issued by or under the direct control of Producer, then Artist shall also receive credit in the same item of paid advertising, in substantially the same size of type and style as that accorded such other cast member (subject to customary exclusions). All other aspects of such credit shall be within Producer's sole discretion. No casual or inadvertent failure of Producer, or any failure of any third party, to accord credit hereunder shall constitute a breach of this Agreement. Upon Producer's receipt of written notice from Artist specifying any failure to give Artist any credit required hereunder, Producer shall use reasonable business efforts to cure such failure on a prospective basis only. Under no circumstances shall Producer be required to recall any prints or advertising materials. Producer shall use good faith efforts to notify the Network or any other applicable third party of the credit requirements hereunder; provided, however, that any inadvertent failure to do so shall not constitute a breach hereunder.

> When it comes to unscripted talent agreements, the credit provision will often be short, if mentioned at all apart from the standard terms and conditions. The credit provision may be as simple as "all credits, if any, shall be at the sole discretion of the network and subject to network policy." In most cases, the producer will not be a SAG-AFTRA signatory; therefore there are no minimum credit requirements. Without the guild, the parties are free to negotiate for whatever credit provision both parties are willing to agree to.

If the talent is a celebrity, or has some leverage, the talent's representative should try to negotiate for better credit guarantees and protections. If the talent is the star of the show, he or she will want a guarantee that the credit is in first position (i.e. the first on-camera talent credit that is aired on screen) on a single card (i.e. not shared with any other credit) in a size and style of type no less favorable that of any other on-camera talent's credit. The talent will want to further request that his or her credit is included in any form of paid advertising ("paid ads") issued by or under the control of the producer and/or network, or at the very least, if any other on-camera talent is accorded credit in paid ads, the talent will also be accorded credit in paid ads.

If the talent's representative is able to negotiate for credit improvements, the representative should also negotiate for protections to ensure that their client actually receives the credit as negotiated. The representative will almost always ask for a contractual requirement or good faith efforts to notify the network or any other third party of the credit requirements provided in the talent attachment agreement. For further protection, the talent will request what is known as "prospective cure" – upon the producer's receipt of written notice from the talent specifying a failure to give credit pursuant to the terms of the talent agreement, the producer agrees to use reasonable efforts to cure the failure on a prospective basis. Even if the producer agrees to both of the aforementioned guarantees, the producer will always qualify them by stating that any failure to notify or failure to cure will not be considered a breach of the agreement.

13. <u>Travel and Expenses</u>: If Artist is required to travel in connection with production of the Series to a location more than seventy-five (75) miles from Artist's primary residence, Producer will furnish Artist with business class airfare (on an if used, if available basis), reasonable hotel accommodations, non-exclusive ground transportation to and from airports (shared only with above-the-line personnel), midsize rental car or ground transportation, at Producer's election (which rental car may also take the place of ground transportation to and from airports) and a Fifty Dollar ($50) per diem for each day while Artist is rendering services as required on location during production of the Series. All such travel arrangements shall be controlled by Producer. Notwithstanding the foregoing, Producer shall furnish Artist with roundtrip business class air transportation (on an if available, if used basis), reasonable hotel accommodations

(room and tax only), non exclusive ground transportation shared only with above-the-line personnel), and a per diem of Fifty Dollars ($50) for each day while Artist is rendering in-person ancillary services as required by Producer outside of production periods for any cycle of the Series for which Producer exercises an option hereunder. If Artist does not reside within one hundred (100) miles of the Los Angeles, California area and relocated to provide services for the Series, Producer will pay Artist a one-time relocation fee of Seven Thousand Five Hundred Dollars ($7,500).

In the event that the producer or network requires the talent to travel (usually between 50-100 miles away from the talent's home), the terms of the talent's travel will be pre-negotiated in the talent agreement. In most instances, the producer will only agree to ground transportation, a reasonable per diem, one coach class round-trip airline ticket, and lodging if an overnight stay is required (all subject to network requirements and the budget of the series). The talent's representative will typically ask for first-class exclusive ground transportation, a minimum per diem (usually $65-$100), first class round-trip airfare, and a hotel suite or a room at a hotel rated 4 stars or better. Of course, the talent's precedent, celebrity status and leverage, if any, will govern where the parties land on this issue.

If the agreement is not governed by SAG-AFTRA, there are no minimum protections for the client. As a starting point for negotiations, the talent representative should refer to the SAG-AFTRA rules and try to negotiate for the same travel guidelines and per diem that would be followed if the producer was a SAG-AFTRA signatory. For instance, under the SAG-AGRA rules, coach class travel may be provided on domestic flights of less than 1000 airline miles, otherwise business class is required, and if business class air is unavailable, the talent must be provided with first class travel.

Despite the talent's representatives best efforts, however, the producer and network will not want to be contractually obligated to provide better travel without a good reason to do so. Moreover, if the series features an ensemble cast, the producer and network will want to keep the travel the same for all of the on-camera talent. There is nothing that will make the talent angrier than getting on a plane to travel with the rest of the cast and finding that they are the only person in coach. This can often be solved, however, by an assurance that all travel will be provided on a no less favorable basis than any other cast member receiving travel.

Of note, if the unscripted show is a docu-series, the talent will likely only be required to travel for promotion of the show, and it is extremely unlikely that the talent will be required to relocate to provide services on the series. However, if the talent is the host or judge of the unscripted program relocation is much more likely. For instance, Heidi Klum lives in Los Angeles, but multiple seasons of Project Runway were filmed in New York. In this instance, Heidi may have received a relocation fee so that she could set up a home in New York during filming. The producer may have also paid for plane tickets for her children and other perks to assist in making the transition to living in New York easier for her.

13A. <u>Hair, Makeup, and Wardrobe</u>: Producer will provide Artist with wardrobe and hair and makeup assistance for the Series as determined in Producer's sole discretion within Producer's budgetary parameters.

The talent's representative will almost always ask the producer to provide the talent with hair, makeup, and wardrobe services in connection with the talent's services on the pilots and series. The talent will also want approval over his or her hair, makeup, and wardrobe, or at the very least, meaningful consultation with respect to talent's overall "look." In the alternative, the celebrity may request a hair, makeup, and wardrobe line item in the production budget so that the talent can hire their personal stylists whom they are comfortable working with. For A-level talent, the producer may further agree that the talent will be allowed to keep all of the wardrobe items worn or used by the talent (with the exception of rented and/or promotional wardrobe items that must be returned) when the wardrobe items are no longer required for additional photography. For a celebrity, host, or judge, the producer will almost always agree to provide some or all of the talent's hair, makeup, and wardrobe requests.

13B. <u>Series Rules</u>: Artist agrees to be bound by the series rules ("Series Rules") which rules may change from time to time as determined in Producer's sole discretion. Artist acknowledges that Artist has been provided a copy of the Series Rules and affirms that Artist understands and agrees to follow and obey such Series Rules and all of Producer's directions and instructions in all matters. Producer's decisions on all conditions and rules governing the Series shall be within Producer's sole control and shall be final and binding in all respects and shall not be subject to challenge or appeal.

Depending on the type of unscripted series being produced, the talent may be required to follow specific rules. If the series is a game or competition show, the rules are particularly important because a violation of the rules could equate to a violation of the law. For instance, it is a federal offense punishable by fine and/or imprisonment for anyone to rig the outcome of a television show with the intent to deceive the viewing public (elements of how these laws were developed and the consequences for breaking these laws were portrayed in the critically acclaimed 1994 movie *Quiz Show*). The talent should ensure that he or she has received, read, and understood the series rules before signing any talent agreement with such a provision.

14. <u>Standards of Performance; Consultation Rights</u>: Artist's services will be rendered either alone or in cooperation with other persons in such manner as Producer may reasonably direct, under the instructions and in strict accordance with the controls and schedules established by Producer's authorized representatives and at the times, places, and in the manner reasonably required by said representatives, subject to the terms of this Agreement. Such services shall be of a quality consistent with first-class industry standards and shall be rendered in an artistic, conscientious, efficient, and punctual manner to Artist's best ability and with full regard to the careful, efficient, economical, and expeditious production of the Series and policies established by Producer (including, without limitation, the terms and conditions of Producer's equal employment policies), it being understood that Producer's production of the Series involves matters of discretion to be exercised by Producer in respect to art and taste, and Artist's services and the manner of rendition thereof are to be governed by Producer.

If the talent is the star of a docu-series or is a celebrity with a pre-established brand, it will likely be very important to the talent that he or she be entitled to a right of meaningful consultation with respect to all creative decisions concerning the series (including changes in the series rules in section 13, if applicable). The producer and network will

REALITY TELEVISION CONTRACTS

only agree to this if absolutely necessary to secure the services of the talent. Even if the producer includes a meaningful consultation right in the agreement, the producer's decision will be final in the event of a disagreement.

In most instances, however, the producer and/or network will not contractually agree to meaningful consultation and all of the talent's on-camera services will be rendered at the reasonable discretion of the producer. In this regard, all matters of discretion exercised by the producer and/or network in regards to the art and taste of the series, the filming schedules and locations, and any other services required by the producer will be final. The talent will be expected to carry out the producer's and/or network's requests to the best of his or her ability and always in an efficient and conscientious manner.

15. <u>Remedies</u>: See Chapter 2.

16. <u>Federal Communications Act</u>: Artist acknowledges that Artist is aware of Section 508 of the Federal Communications Act making it a criminal offense for any person, in connection with the production or preparation of any television program, to accept or pay any money, services, or other valuable consideration for the inclusion of any "plug," reference, product identification, or other matter as a part of such program unless such acceptance or payment is disclosed in the manner required by law. Artist further understands that it is the policy of Producer not to permit the acceptance or payment of such consideration and that any such acceptance or payment will be cause for immediate termination of this Agreement. Without limiting the foregoing, Artist expressly agrees that Artist will not accept or pay, or agree to pay, any such consideration.

The network is the gatekeeper of any and all products or services that are promoted on a television series. The networks typically have entire departments devoted solely to the administration of in-show product placements. Although this law is meant to protect consumers, the network benefits as it relates to the talent—it ensures that the talent cannot legally agree to anything that conflicts with network-initiated product placement agreements.

If the talent has a pre-existing agreement to promote products or services, this should be disclosed from the outset so that the network's promotions department can decide how it should be handled. For instance, if the talent has a pre-existing agreement to wear a certain clothing brand whenever he or she appears on television, the network may choose to enter into a separate agreement with the clothing brand that provides a network benefit for the additional exposure and clarifies how the promotional consideration will be disclosed pursuant to the federal guidelines.

17. <u>Publicity/Confidentiality</u>: Any publicity, paid advertisements, press notices, or other information with respect to this Agreement and any of the projects and terms referred to herein shall be under the sole control of Producer. Therefore, Artist shall not consent to and/or authorize any person or entity to release such information without the express prior written approval of Producer. The foregoing shall not be deemed to prohibit Artist from issuing personal publicity concerning Artist incidentally mentioning the Series, providing the same is of a non-confidential nature, and does not mention the Series, any personnel engaged in connection therewith, or Producer in an unfavorable or derogatory manner. Artist shall, at all times, keep in confidence and shall not use for Artist or others, other than in connection with the business or affairs of Producer, or divulge to others (excluding Artist's representatives), any information, knowledge, or data of Producer or relating to the Series that Artist knows (or reasonably could be expected to know) is secret or confidential, unless authorized by Producer, or required by law, and except to Artist's business representatives or for "quote" purposes, or to Artist's attorney, agent, or as required by court order, provided such disclosure is on a confidential basis and subject to the terms of this Paragraph 18. Except as provided herein, Artist shall have no right to refer to the Series or to use the

name, logo, or other marks related to _____, the Series, Producer, or the Network without Producer's prior written approval in each instance. Any violation of the terms of this paragraph by Artist may be deemed by Producer to be a material breach by Artist of this Agreement. The covenants set forth in this paragraph shall survive the termination of this Agreement. Producer shall meaningfully consult in good faith with Artist regarding the initial press release issued by Producer regarding Artist's engagement hereunder.

The confidentiality clause is perhaps the most important term to the producer and network. If details or the outcome of an unscripted program are revealed prior to airing, it could substantially hinder the success of the show. The producer and network will go to great lengths to keep situations and outcomes of a series a secret from the public.

In some instances (typically if the unscripted series is a competition or game show) the producer will include a steep "liquidated damages" clause to ensure that the talent is incentivized to keep their mouths shut after filming (i.e., the talent will owe the producer a pre-determined dollar amount, usually upwards of a million dollars, if the talent breaches the confidentiality agreement. This amount is meant to compensate the producer for damages that would be too difficult to calculate). It is rumored that each contestant on the *Bachelor/Bachelorette* signs an on-camera talent agreement with a five-million-dollar liquidated damages clause – for *The Amazing Race*, ten million. Once a contestant is kicked off of the series, the producers sometimes hold the talent at an undisclosed location for the duration of filming. The producers may also shoot fake scenes or alternative endings to further protect the results of the program. Upon returning home or at the conclusion of filming, the producer will send letters to the talent reminding them of their continued confidentiality obligations and the potential consequences of revealing details about the series that have not yet aired.

Despite these efforts, the talent may still choose to reveal confidential information about the series, and the producer's and network's only recourse may be to sue the talent or the person who obtained the confidential information. Here are a few examples of how a breach of the confidentiality provision has played out in the courts:

In 2001, former *Survivor* contestant Stacy Stillman sued CBS and the Survivor Entertainment Group (SEG). In her lawsuit, Stacy revealed confidential information about the program. In response to the lawsuit (and her discussions with the press about her allegations), CBS and SEG were permitted to proceed with a breach of contract lawsuit against Stacy to enforce the five-million-dollar liquidated damages provision of her on-camera agreement. A similar situation occurred in 2010 when participants on the program *Ultimate Women's Challenge* sued the producers of the series alleging that they had not been paid money they were owed. In response, the producer counter-sued the contestants (and the contestants' attorney!) for revealing confidential information about the program.

NZK Productions and Horizon Alternative Television, a division of Warner Bros, has sued "Reality" Steve Carbone (of realitysteve.com) twice for allegedly enticing *Bachelor* and *Bachelorette* contestants into revealing spoilers about the show.

In 2010 the BBC unsuccessfully sued HarperCollins to stop the publisher from revealing the identity of the masked stunt driver on "Top Gear."

25. Cast Insurance: Producer may, at Producer's expense, obtain life, health, or other insurance covering Artist for Producer's benefit, and such insurance may be taken in Producer's and/or Artist's names. In connection therewith, subject to Artist's professional availability if outside of production periods, Artist shall submit to any reasonably required examinations (provided Artist may have Artist's own physician present at such examinations at Artist's expense), and shall correctly and promptly prepare, sign, and deliver any required applications or other documents. Artist shall have the right to have Artist's own physician present at any such examinations, at Artist's sole cost. The results of any such examination shall be kept confidential except to the extent necessary to disclose to the insurance carrier and production personnel on a need-to-know basis, and except as required by law or court order. Failure to complete such examination as provided above shall constitute a material breach hereof. Artist warrants and represents that Artist is in good health and has no known condition that would prevent Producer from obtaining insurance at premium rates normal to Artist's age and sex, without any unusual exclusions or limitations, provided Producer shall first afford Artist an opportunity to pay any excess premium. In the event Producer is unable to obtain cast insurance, or in the event that Artist fails to

observe all terms and conditions necessary to continue such insurance in effect, Producer shall be entitled to terminate this Agreement and shall have no further obligations to Artist; provided Producer shall not be entitled to terminate this Agreement with respect to any production cycle after Artist's services in connection with principal photography of that particular production cycle have commenced.

ADDITIONAL TERMS

The parties are always free to negotiate for additional provisions other than those that are typically included in an on-camera talent agreement. Other terms that the parties may agree to include the following:

Ratings Bonus / Production Bonus: The talent may ask for a production bonus in the second and subsequent cycles that will be paid whereby the talent receives additional compensation if the network orders production of an additional cycle, the talent's option is exercised, and the talent actually renders and completes all services on the applicable cycle.

The talent may also ask for a ratings bonus. The ratings bonus may be structured in one of two ways: (1) when the Nielsen rating meets the applicable ratings threshold, a bonus becomes payable based on the highest threshold achieved or (2) if the season's average rating meets or exceeds the average rating from the previous cycle. This bonus is only paid once (i.e., it cannot be compounded). If the talent is attempting to negotiate for more money after the show has become a success, the network and producer will be much more likely to agree to a ratings bonus.

Contingent Compensation: If the talent is a celebrity or has made significant creative contributions to the show, the producer may offer the talent a percentage of any contingent compensation paid to the producer (typically between 5 and 20 percent). Because the talent is receiving a piece of any contingent compensation received by the producer, the definition will not likely be negotiable and may even include additional deductions that are taken from the producer's definition.

Producer Credit / Separate Line-Item for Producing Services: If the talent meaningfully contributed to the concept of the program, the series is developed around the talent, and he or she intends to continue to contribute to the creative aspects of the series, the talent may request a producer credit. Even if the talent has, and intends to continue, participating in the foregoing ways, the network will be hesitant to agree to the credit unless the talent has prior credits on television. If warranted, the talent may also ask for a separate line-item in the budget to pay the talent an additional fee for his or her producing services. The talent may further request that he or she be "locked for life" to the series as a producer. If the network will not agree to the credit, the parties often agree that if the talent renders sufficient producing services during the first cycle, he or she will receive a producing credit for the second cycle and all subsequent cycles.

Location Fee: If the producer intends to film at the talent's home, business, or any other property owned or controlled by the talent, the talent may request a separate flat fee for use of all of the talent's property. Of course, the talent will still need to sign a location agreement for each location (see chapter 8); however, no additional fee will be paid.

Publicist Fee: If the talent is a noted celebrity or the show becomes a huge success, the producer may agree to pay a flat fee for a publicist to represent the talent for each cycle of the series.

Security for Personal Appearances: If the talent is a major celebrity, he or she may require security be provided at all public promotional appearances. If the talent has a security guard that he or she is comfortable with, the parties may include a contractual obligation that provides the preferred security guard's name as well as travel and a fee.

Hidden Camera: The talent will typically request an acknowledgement that there will be no hidden cameras used in the Series, or that if hidden cameras are used, they will not be used in any place where the talent would have a reasonable expectation of privacy (e.g., their home, bedroom, bathroom, shower, designated changing area, vehicle, etc.). If the producer intends to use hidden cameras or is not willing to agree contractually that hidden cameras will not be used, the producer may agree to point out every camera to the talent at any production location prior to filming. The producer may further agree that the producer will not film phone conversations or meetings if they relate to confidential business matters.

Knock Before Entering: The talent may request a contractual requirement that the producer will knock first and wait before entering the talent's bedroom.

Filming Artist's Child(ren): If the talent has a child, the talent may require a contractual obligation from the producer stating that the talent's child/children will not be filmed without the talent's approval in each instance. Of course, if a minor is used in the program, a contract or appearance release must be signed by the minor and the minor's parent or guardian.

Assumption of Risk / Hazardous Activity: Depending on the nature of the unscripted series, the producer may require that the talent affirm that he or she is in excellent mental and physical health and that he or she does not know of any reason that he or she cannot participate in the activity. The producer will require that the talent further affirm that he or she assumes all of the physical or other risk associated with performing the hazardous activity and that the talent releases the producer from any and all claims, demands, causes of action, damages, etc. directly or indirectly relating to or arising from the talent's participation in the potentially hazardous activity.

DVD Copies: To the extent a DVD of the series becomes commercially available to the public, the talent will often ask for a contractual requirement to provide one copy of the DVD release of the series for his or her personal use.

Nudity: If the talent is a celebrity, he or she will likely ask that the contract clarify that the producer will not use any material that depicts the talent nude without the talent's prior written consent.

The producer will always take out a cast-insurance policy. If the talent dies, is injured, or becomes ill, the insurance company will reimburse the producer for any additional costs resulting from the talent's incapacity that are incurred to complete principal photography. In order to qualify for this insurance, each cast member who will be covered must submit to a medical/physical examination. At the talent's option, and at the talent's expense, the talent will always have the right to have his or her own physician present during the examination.

The talent is usually asked to affirm that producer will be able to obtain insurance coverage at the premium rate for a person of the talent's same age and sex. If the talent does not qualify for the typical standard premium rate, the producer has the option to terminate the agreement. If this language is included, the talent representative should try to have the language deleted. If the producer refuses, the talent should ask for the option to pay any excess premiums. That said, if the talent has a particular ailment, injury, etc. that they know in advance will make them subject to higher premiums, the talent should make the producer aware as soon as possible so that the producer can decide whether they want to continue with the talent and who will pay for the excess.

In the case of reality television, where the series often reveals the most private aspects of a person's life, the talent should ensure that the language in the talent agreement obligates the results of any examination to be kept confidential, except to the extent they must be reported to an insurance carrier or to production or network personnel. Most importantly, the talent should confirm via the talent agreement that the results of any examination cannot be incorporated into the series without the express approval of the talent.

19. <u>No Obligation</u>: See Chapter 2.

20. <u>Representations and Warranties</u>: See Chapter 2.

21. <u>Indemnity</u>: See Chapter 2.

22. <u>Assignment</u>: See Chapter 2.

23. <u>Breach and Incapacity</u>: See Chapter 2.

24. <u>Force Majeure</u>: See Chapter 2.

25. <u>Morals</u>: See Chapter 2.

26. <u>Insurance</u>: See Chapter 2.

27. <u>Non-Guild</u>: See Chapter 2.

28. <u>Arbitration</u>: See Chapter 2.

29. <u>Miscellaneous</u>: No waiver by either party hereto of any condition or provision of this Agreement shall be considered a waiver of any other condition or provision of this Agreement or of the same conditions or provision at another time. Should any provision hereof be found invalid, in whole or in part, it shall not affect the validity or enforceability of any other provision hereof or of that provision insofar as it is not invalid or unenforceable. This Agreement shall bind and inure to the benefit of the parties hereto and each of their respective successors, assigns, heirs, legal representatives, administrators, executors, and guardians.

30. <u>Entire Agreement</u>: This instrument includes the entire under-standing of the parties with respect to its subject matter, and all

prior agreements, warranties, and representations with respect to such subject matter have been merged herein. No representations or warranties have been made other than those expressly provided for herein. This Agreement may not be modified except by a written instrument by both parties.

IN WITNESS WHEREOF, the parties hereto have executed this Agreement as of the date written below.

ACCEPTED AND AGREED:

Producer   **Artist**

_____   By: _____
NAME, President   **NAME**

DEAL POINT CHECKLIST
On-Air Talent Agreement

1. Satisfaction of Conditions Precedent
2. First Series Year and Subsequent Series Years
   - Series Exercise Date
   - Number of Subsequent Options
   - Episodic Fee and Per Cycle Increases to the Artist's Episodic Fee
   - Episodic Guarantee
3. Exclusivity
4. Services included in the Artist's Episodic Fee vs. Services that Require Additional Compensation
5. In-Show Integrations
6. Name, Likeness, and Biography Approval
7. Merchandising
   - Approval over Merchandising Use
   - Royalty for Merchandising Use
8. Credit
   - Credit Guarantee / Position / Single or Shared Card / Size and Style Tie
   - Paid Advertising
   - Prospective Cure
   - Third Party Notice of Credit Obligations
9. Travel
10. Hair, Makeup, and Wardrobe
11. Series Rules
12. Series Consultation Rights
13. Confidentiality

14. Cast Insurance
15. Miscellaneous
    - Ratings Bonus / Production Bonus
    - Contingent Compensation
    - Producer Credit / Separate Line-Item for Producing Services
    - Location Fee
    - Publicist Fee
    - Security for Personal Appearances
    - Hidden Camera
    - Knock and Enter Policy
    - Filming Artist's Child(ren)
    - Assumption of Risk / Hazardous Activity
    - Nudity
    - DVD Copy of Series

7

Production Services Agreement

The networks and the established production companies are the primary players involved with reality television shows that have an *opportunity* to be produced and broadcast. Content across platforms is reliant on the parties that make the content (production companies) and the parties that distribute the content (networks). If a network (more likely a network subsidiary) provides an order for a show—that is, agrees to fund a specific number of episodes—then the production company is required to negotiate and enter a "Production Services Agreement" with the network. The sample production services agreement below is between an entity that is a network subsidiary—that is, a company wholly owned by the channel—which will own the show and be responsible for the production company's and executive producer's compliance with the terms of this agreement. These contracts are generally entered by a network subsidiary because the television channels that broadcast reality television programs are owned and operated as divisions and subsidiaries of international mass media companies. For example, the channels MTV, Nickelodeon, and CMT are channels owned by Viacom Media Networks, which is a company that is owned by Viacom, Inc. For legal and tax purposes, each channel creates and owns many subsidiary companies that the channels use to produce individual television shows.

As we covered in other chapters, the production company has previously entered into an agreement with the owner of the rights to the show and has most likely created a sizzle reel and other development items to assist their pitches to the networks to attract an offer for the show. The production company is the primary party involved in the production and delivery of a show to the network and the original creator(s) or producer of the content is usually included in this contract, specifying the role of such creator(s) or producer in the production of the show and the basic terms controlling the services the creator(s) or producer will provide to the show in exchange for transferring all rights in and to the property.

As of DATE

Production Company Name
Address
Address
Executive Producer's Name

RE: **"Production Services Agreement" With Production Company Name ("Production Company") f/s/o Executive Producer ("Artist") regarding currently entitled project "Unscripted Show" ("Project")**

The following sets forth the terms of the Production Services Agreement ("Agreement") between Subsidiary Entity of Network ("Network Subsidiary") and Production Company regarding an unscripted thirty-minute television program currently entitled "Unscripted Show" (the "Project," sometimes also referred to as the

"Series") based on a concept created and/or developed by Production Company ("Concept") for the production services of Production Company and the producing services of Executive Producer.

> The production company name is the production company that will produce and deliver the show to the network. Networks most often work with established production companies that have previously produced and delivered shows to that specific network because the network is expending large sums of money and is entrusting the parties with delivering the show on time and on budget. Examples of established reality television production companies include: 3 Ball Entertainment (*Extreme Weight Loss*, *Bar Rescue*), Original Productions (*Deadliest Catch*, *Storage Wars*), and No Coast Originals (*Fast N' Loud*, *Salvage City*).
>
> The Executive Producer "Artist" is often the party that developed the show or at least attached himself or herself with other people who developed the show. In any case, this party has agreed in a previous contract to transfer any and all rights to the production company upon the happening of a specific event, usually an order or sale to a network.
>
> As mentioned above, the networks most often use a subsidiary to enter the agreement with the production company. Networks own many subsidiaries to segregate funds and liability for different endeavors (such as television shows, movies, gaming, etc.).
>
> The production company may own all of the rights to the show because the show was one that was developed and created within the production company, or the production company may own the rights to the show because it previously entered a separate agreement with the rights owner; for example, an agreement such as a "Collaboration Agreement."

1. Conditions Precedent. Network Subsidiary's obligations in this Agreement are subject to the satisfaction of all of the following:

> Conditions precedent means that unless all of the items listed in this paragraph are satisfied, then the network is not obligated to fulfill any of its promises in the Production Services Agreement. There are certain factors that are assumed during the pitches and negotiations of reality television shows. One assumption is that the party or parties presenting the show actually own the rights to the show. The documents that prove who is the owner of intellectual property (such as a reality television show) are called the

"chain-of-title. Another common requirement is that the production company deliver fully completed and fully executed forms required to comply with all government and other regulatory bodies, such as tax and immigration forms.

2. Development Services. Production Company and Artist shall receive an all-inclusive fee of Eight Thousand Dollars ($8,000), payable upon the Network Subsidiary's receipt of the Development Delivery Items (defined below). Production Company and Artist agree to provide Network Subsidiary all pre-existing materials regarding the Concept in addition to providing development services for the Concept and Project as customarily provided by production companies and producers of unscripted television programs in New York and Los Angeles including, but not limited to, providing the budget (subject to Network Subsidiary approval) and a tentative schedule (subject to Network Subsidiary approval) for the Project (collectively, the "Development Delivery Items").

The all-inclusive development fee is negotiable, but it is usually a small amount between $5,000 and $15,000. Of course, certain shows, producers, and production companies can and do command more than this range of fee, but producers and production companies usually don't want to stall or lose the overall order of the show because they demand more upfront development money. What the production company and producers do want is a show that has many episodes over many cycles, which is how they can maximize the amount of money they can make from a reality television show.

3. Series Services.
    (a) Pilot. Network Subsidiary hereby orders and Production Company agrees to deliver an eighteen (18) to twenty-two (22) minute not-for-air pilot ("Pilot") and a three (3) to five (5) minute "sales presentation reel" (as the term is generally understood in the North American television industry, also sometimes termed a "sizzle reel") of the Project. In consideration of delivery of the

Pilot and sales presentation reel to Network Subsidiary and the full performance of Production Company's and Artist's obligations in this Agreement, Network Subsidiary shall provide One Hundred Thousand Dollars ($100,000.00) ("Pilot Fee") upon full execution of this Agreement. The Pilot Fee shall be inclusive of all development and/or production costs incurred to deliver the Pilot and sales presentation reel. Production Company shall be solely responsible for any and all Pilot and/or sales presentation reel overages (that is, in excess of $100,000.00). Production Company will deliver to Network Subsidiary the sales presentation reel no later than _____, 20__ and the Pilot no later than _____, 20__, both subject to *force majeure*.

The amount of the Pilot Fee is an all-in amount and is subject to negotiation. For half-hour shows the amounts are between $35,000 and $125,000 for the delivery of the pilot and sales presentation reel. An all-in amount means that all costs required to deliver the pilot and the sales presentation reel are the *sole* responsibility of the Production Company. This is one reason that networks usually only work with established production companies, and often will only with work with production companies that have produced previous reality shows for the network. The Production Company, on the other hand, is taking a risk that the delivered elements can be produced at the all-in budget amount and at a quality level acceptable to the network. Again, these are further reasons why reality television producing is primarily within the control of established production companies. Experience is required to create an accurate budget and to execute the production on time and on budget. Further, an experienced production company often has working capital or access to lenders if there are production problems and the pilot goes over budget. It should be noted that any line-item fees that could be payable to the Production Company and Artist would have to be paid from the all-in amount. It is not uncommon for production companies and producers to end up with no payment from the production of the pilot and sales presentation reel.

(b) First Cycle. Subject to Network Subsidiary's approval of the budget for the Series (Network Subsidiary hereby acknowledges approval of the budget for the First Cycle, as defined in this Agreement, and which is attached hereto as Exhibit __), and the conditions precedent set forth in Section 1, Network Subsidiary hereby engages Production Company to provide production services and to furnish Artist's executive producer services in connection with the first cycle of the Series, on a "pay-or-play" basis (with respect to the fee payable for Production Company's production services and Artist's executive producer services, and subject to Network Subsidiary's rights in the event of default, disability, or *force majeure*), with a minimum guarantee of six (6) episodes ("First Cycle"). Principal photography shall commence no later than _____, 20__ and be completed by _____, 20__.

The budget for a reality show depends on the type of show. For example, *The Millionaire Matchmaker* is a show that would have a production budget between $50,000 and $125,000 per <u>half hour</u> episode. At the opposite end of the budget spectrum, a show like *American Idol* would have an all-in budget <u>per hour</u> of approximately $800,000 to $1 million for the first season. Other types of shows will have a budget between these high and low budgets.

If the Network Subsidiary orders a Pilot, they most often will then make the First Cycle subject to an option. That is, "Subject to Network Subsidiary's approval of the budget for the Series and the conditions precedent set forth in Section 1, the Network Subsidiary shall have the exclusive, irrevocable option to order a First Cycle." The Network Subsidiary's approval could also be subject to its approval of the on-air talent that is cast in the Pilot.

(c) Project Options.

   i.   Network Subsidiary shall have the exclusive, irrevocable option to order from Production Company up to a maximum of forty-four (44) total episodes ("Additional

Episode Option") per the First Cycle and each Cycle (defined below), provided that Network Subsidiary must order a minimum of six (6) episodes from Production Company at any time that Network Subsidiary exercises an Additional Episode Option.

> The minimum number of episodes is open to negotiation. The network would like to commit the minimum amount of resources to a show until it is certain that the show has enough viewers to continue spending the money. The production company would like to increase the number of episodes for the obvious reason that it can make more money, but also because a lesser number of episodes makes it more difficult for a production company to get a full production up and running. Further, for the same reasons, a production company would like to have the network agree that the network's option to demand additional episodes be contingent on the production company being in continuous production.

ii.   The budget for each additional episode shall not exceed Seventy Thousand Dollars ($70,000.00) per additional episode ("Additional Episode Budget") and shall be subject to Network Subsidiary's prior sole approval on a line-by-line item basis.

> The Network Subsidiary will often add that the additional episode budget shall be subject to downward adjustment for larger Series episode orders. The Production Company will want to negotiate and add that in any case the Network Subsidiary will be responsible for any additional costs caused by industry, guild, or other negotiated increases. Further, the parties should agree that any costs related to on-air talent that is affected by any guild requirements or for any other reason, including but not limited to re-negotiation with on-air talent regarding previously agreed upon on-air talent fees, shall be in addition to the Additional Episode Budget.
>
> Usually, the parties will agree to negotiate in good faith regarding the delivery schedule of any such additional episode.

iii. Further, Production Company and Artist shall receive a line item fee for service provided on the additional episode(s), such fee to be equal to the per-episode fee received in connection with the initial order for such Cycle upon which additional episodes are ordered. For clarity, such 10% fee shall not be 10% of the Additional Episode Budget but shall be 10% of the amount that is the product of (x) the number of episodes in the initial order for such Cycle upon which additional episodes are ordered and (y) the total Budget of the initial order for the Cycle upon which additional episodes are ordered.

The Production Company will want to be careful that it is not 10% of the Additional Episode Budget, which is often lower than original Budget.

The Production Company will also want to add that Network Subsidiary shall reimburse Production Company for all actual, reasonable, avoidable out-of-pocket costs and expenses directly attributable to Production Company's inability to remain in continuous production due to Network Subsidiary's failure to order additional episodes in a timely manner. It is advisable to add that at the beginning of each Cycle that the Production Company be required to notify Network Subsidiary in writing of the date by which Network Subsidiary must order additional episodes so that Production Company shall be able to remain in continuous production, and Production Company shall revise such date as necessary during production to reflect changed circumstances.

iv. Additional Cycles. Subsequent to the First Cycle the Network Subsidiary shall have the exclusive, irrevocable option to order successive cycles (each a "Cycle") of the Series for which Production Company shall provide production services and executive producing services of Artist. Network Subsidiary shall have six (6) consecutive and dependent options (each a "Cycle Option"). Network Subsidiary and Production Company agree that

Production Company shall have no less than twelve weeks prior to the delivery of the first episode of any additional Cycle unless the parties agree to a time period for pre-production and production that is less than twelve weeks. Subject to neither Production Company nor Artist being in material breach of this Agreement and subject to the Standard Terms and Conditions attached hereto as Exhibit A, Production Company and Artist shall be engaged on a "pay-or-play" basis for a line-item fee for production services and executive producing services for each such Cycle of the Series, and the minimum number of episodes guaranteed to Production Company and Artist on a pay-or-play basis shall be six (6) episodes. Nothing in this Agreement shall hinder or impede Network Subsidiary's sole, unilateral right to order more episodes than six (6) episodes regarding any Cycle or to increase an order from an initial number of additional episodes within a Cycle. Network Subsidiary shall provide Production Company written notice of each Cycle Option no later than sixteen (16) weeks after the initial exhibition of the last episode of the Series produced for the immediately preceding Cycle and no later than twelve (12) weeks prior to the delivery of the first episode of any additional Cycle unless the parties agree to a time period for pre-production and production that is less than twelve (12) weeks.

Often the Additional Cycle options are drafted with the following language: "additional, separate, exclusive, consecutive, irrevocable, dependent options." This language will be applied to each show according to the Network Subsidiary's needs.

The terms regarding the Additional Cycle are negotiable, but within the context of the specific show. For example, a successful production company would like to reduce the number of option for Additional Cycles to two or three; the Network Subsidiary would want at least six, but may ask for more. The Production Company is concerned about how long it will have to deliver additional shows, so it will want at least 12 weeks to produce the shows and at least 16 weeks of notice from the Network Subsidiary that it wants more shows. In addition, the Production Company will want a reasonable number of additional episodes for it to be efficient to produce more episodes, that is, at least six, but preferably a minimum order of 12 episodes. The Production Company will want to also agree to have mutual approval over the production schedule with the Network Subsidiary.

(d) Budget. Production Company shall prepare a budget for the Pilot and the First Cycle which shall be One Hundred Thousand Dollars ($100,000.00) for the Pilot ("Pilot Budget") and Seven Hundred and Fifty-Five Thousand Dollars ($755,000.00) for the First Cycle order of six (6) episodes ("First Cycle Budget"). The Network Subsidiary shall have final, unilateral approval on a line-by-line-item basis over both the Pilot Budget and the First Cycle Budget; a copy of each is attached hereto as Exhibit B. Network Subsidiary shall provide payment of the Pilot Budget and First Cycle Budget as follows: (i) 50% upon commencement of pre-production; (ii) 20% upon commencement of production; and (iii) 30% upon delivery of Delivery Requirements in accordance with the terms attached hereto as Exhibit C. Each instance that a Network Subsidiary exercises a Cycle Option, if any, the budget for each subsequent Cycle shall be an amount up to five percent (5%) more than the budget of the preceding Cycle ("Subsequent Cycle Budget"). Provided that neither Production Company nor Artist are in breach of this Agreement, Network Subsidiary shall provide payment for each Subsequent Cycle Budget as follows: (i) 20% upon commencement of pre-production; (ii) thereafter on a bi-weekly, pro rata basis, except for the final 20%; (iii) 20% upon delivery of Delivery Requirements in accordance with the terms provided by Network Subsidiary. The Pilot Budget, First Cycle

Budget and each Subsequent Cycle Budget shall be "all–in" budgets, that is, each shall be inclusive of all costs and expenses to prepare, produce, complete, and deliver each of the Pilot, First Cycle, and each subsequent Cycle to Network Subsidiary in accordance with this Agreement.

The Pilot Budget, the First Cycle Budget and number of episodes, the payment schedule, and the percentage increase of the budget for each subsequent cycle are negotiable, but depend upon the specific show, as described above.

The Production Company should negotiate and add that such an "all-in" budget shall not include any overage costs approved by Network Subsidiary, any delay costs created by Network Subsidiary, any breaches by Network Subsidiary, and also not include any overhead charges by Network Subsidiary.

(e) To the extent that any Network Subsidiary personnel or in-house departments perform any services or provide any goods regarding the Series (or if the Network Subsidiary exercises its takover rights in accordance with Section 9 of this Agreement), then such goods and/or services shall not be included in the Budget (as defined in Section 3 d.) and such amounts shall not be reflected as a line item in the Budget.

The Production Company will want to negotiate and add that this right is exercisable after meaningful consultation with Production Company, and also that it shall not affect Producer's Series Fee. The Production Company will want the Network Subsidiary to agree that cash flow for any Cycle is to be adjusted by the Network Subsidiary based on monthly cost reports submitted by Production Company.

(f) Overages/Underages. Production Company is responsible for all costs and expenses incurred in producing and delivering the Pilot, First Cycle, and any subsequent Cycle in excess of the Budget (i.e., "overages").

The Production Company should be able to negotiate and receive certain limiting terms. For example, it should request that the following not be considered "overages": (1) any and all costs or expenses incurred as requested by Network Subsidiary outside the approved Budget, provided that any such cost and expense is not caused by or required from Production Company's breach of this Agreement, including but not limited to conforming to the Delivery Requirements; (2) any and all costs as a result of Network Subsidiary's negligence or willful misconduct, including but not limited to delaying or failing to provide Network Subsidiary's approvals in accordance with this Agreement; and (3) any and all costs or expenses that are approved in writing by an authorized representative of Network Subsidiary.

If and to the extent the costs and expenses incurred in producing and delivering the Pilot, First Cycle, and any subsequent Cycle are less than the Budget (i.e, "underages"), then Production Company shall pay such difference to Network Subsidiary. Network Subsidiary shall have the right to offset any undisputed amount of such difference against future license fee or other payments due to Production Company in the event Production Company does not pay such undisputed amount to Network Subsidiary within thirty (30) days of reasonable written demand.

The Production Company would like to negotiate and add that it may retain a certain percentage of the "underages," for example, up to five percent (5%) of the Budget; or a split of "underages" between the Production Company and the Network Subsidiary up to an aggregate amount (for example, up to $50,000) after which the Network Subsidiary retains the "underage" amounts.

Network Subsidiary shall have the right to audit Production Company's books and records with respect to the Series during business hours and upon reasonable prior written notice in accordance with television industry standards and reasonable audit procedures and to be completed within thirty (30) days of commencement.

(g) Production Duties. Production Company and Artist shall provide all production services required in order to produce and
provide delivery of Delivery Requirements (in accordance with
the terms attached hereto as Exhibit C) to the Project and Series
within the time frame specified by Network Subsidiary.

The delivery dates for the first production elements will be agreed upon and added to
this Agreement either in the Agreement or in the Exhibit attached with the Delivery
Requirements. For example, if only the Pilot is ordered, then the delivery date for the Pilot
will be specified and the delivery dates for the subsequent options will remain unspec-
ified until a later date; if the First Cycle is ordered, then the delivery dates for the First
Cycle will be specified. The Production Company will want to carefully review these dates
to ensure that they have sufficient time to deliver the Pilot or First Cycle as required.

Delivery in accordance with this Agreement shall be of the
essence. As soon as available within a reasonable time after
the completion of photography of any episode, Production
Company shall provide Network Subsidiary any and all physical elements reasonably requested by Network Subsidiary for
the creation of advertising and promotional materials.

The expense for creating the promotional materials by Network Subsidiary is usually the
Network Subsidiary's (not the Production Company's) expense.

Production Company will provide the services of Artist in
accordance with the Terms of this Agreement and subject to the
Standard Terms and Conditions attached hereto as Exhibit A,
subject to changes, if any, at the discretion of Network Subsidiary.

The Production Company will want to change this to "as agreed to by the Parties subject
to good faith negotiation."

If there is any conflict between this Agreement and Exhibit A then the terms of this Agreement shall control. Production Company hereby represents, warrants, and agrees to the following: See Chapter 2.

The Network Subsidiary will usually negotiate additional services and content for the Production Company to provide such as deliverables in addition to those required in the Delivery Requirements of an attached Exhibit. For example, agreeing to provide "host wraparounds" (short segments with a host before and after a show); voice-overs; promotional materials; extended programming content; and mini-episodes. If these services and content are required, then the Production Company should negotiate to add that the budget for these items is in addition to the budget for the Series, and agree to the procedure for agreeing to a budget, the Production Company's fees for such services and content, and the terms if the parties can't agree, which is customarily that the Network Subsidiary can engage the services of a third party to create this content and Production Company agrees to cooperate and provide content it has regarding the Series to such third party creator(s).

"Production Duties" to be provided by Production Company and Artist in accordance with this Agreement shall be on a non–exclusive, first priority basis commencing on such date as Network Subsidiary shall designate for the Pilot or any Cycle and continuing through the date that all Delivery Requirements in Exhibit C are satisfied with respect to such Pilot or Cycle.

The Network Subsidiary will want to add that such "first priority basis" is subject to "no services of Artist for third parties or for Artist's own account materially interfering with Artist's obligations to Network Subsidiary under this Agreement." The Production Company and Artist will want to add that at all other times such services are just "non-exclusive."

(h) Clearances. The Production Company, at its sole expense, shall obtain all necessary permissions, licenses, and rights clearances for each and every element in the Series and shall deliver the Series free and clear from any claims, charges, debts, or liens.

The Production Company should negotiate and add that all such clearances shall be a line item in the budget, not to be at the Production Company's sole expense. The Production Company and Network Subsidiary should also carefully review the essential elements of any show to determine if music, artwork, trademarks, celebrity rights, film and television clips, or other elements will better serve the show if they are cleared by, and at the expense of, the Network Subsidiary. This is not customary and the Network Subsidiary's willingness to shoulder certain clearance and costs will be directly proportional to its enthusiasm for airing such show. If a Network Subsidiary is willing to clear certain elements at its own cost, then Production Company should ask Network Subsidiary to indemnify, defend, and hold Production Company harmless from any claims regarding such cleared elements.

(i) Insurance. See Chapter 2.

(j) Series Fee. Production Company and Artist shall receive a fee of 10% of the Budget for the First Cycle ("Series Fee"), such Series Fee to increase four percent (4%) on a cumulative basis for each additional Cycle.

The Network Subsidiary will want to add that the Series Fee shall be paid when production services are actually rendered and completed; the Production Company will want to obtain its fee as early in the process as possible. Usually, there is a compromise to pay a percentage of the fee at milestones such as pre-production, production, and complete delivery. The Production Company and Artist will want the Agreement to state that they are "locked" to the Series; see Section I below.

Other payments to the Production Company that may be negotiated and added include:

1. Production Bonus: An additional amount may be paid to Production Company and Artist for each Cycle that Network Subsidiary exercises a Cycle Option. The amount is usually a flat amount that can range between 2% and 5% of the Budget for the Cycle.

2. Ratings Bonus. It is not often that a Production Company or Artist will have the leverage to ask and receive rating bonuses. However, if the Network Subsidiary agrees to this, such payments will be calculated as a flat fee for performances within a stated demographic above a stated rating point. For

> example, a ratings bonus could pay $25,000 plus $2,500 per tenth of a rating
> point above 2.0 for persons aged 12 to 34 per episode. As a benchmark, the
> first season of *Jersey Shore* reportedly averaged a 2.6 rating for persons aged
> 12 to 34, but its final episode was a 4.8 rating.

(k) Contingent Compensation. Provided that Production Company and Artist are not in material uncured breach of this Agreement, then Production Company shall receive the following Contingent Compensation: (i) ten percent (10%) of one hundred percent (100%) of "Modified Adjusted Gross Receipts" ("MAGR," as defined in "Exhibit _" attached hereto);

> The percentage of contingent compensation is negotiable, but it is commonly between
> 5% and 15%. The Production Company will also want to ask for "most favored nations"
> regarding the percentage and definition of contingent compensation. Most favored
> nations means that if any third party similarly situated or below the Production Company
> receives a greater percentage or a better definition of contingent compensation, then
> the Production Company would also receive such better percentage and/or definition.
>
> The Network Subsidiary sometimes includes that certain revenue—for example, home video
> revenue, merchandising revenue and digital rights revenue—are excluded from the defini-
> tion of MAGR, but are then calculated in accordance to a different definition. This is more
> often the choice of the Network Subsidiary where the definition of MAGR in the "Exhibit"
> attached to this agreement is shorter in length, i.e., two or three pages in length. An exam-
> ple of this "replacement" language is the following: "Merchandising revenue shall not be
> calculated in accordance with "Exhibit __" attached hereto but shall instead be calculated
> as follows: Provided that Production Company and Artist are not in material uncured breach
> of this Agreement, then Production Company shall receive five percent (5%) of one hundred
> percent (100%) of the Merchandising Revenue ("MR"). MR shall be the amount remaining
> after deducting, on a continuing basis, from gross merchandising revenue actually received
> by Network Subsidiary the following in order: (1) a distribution fee of forty percent (40%);
> (2) any and all costs and expenses incurred or paid in the development, manufacturing,
> marketing, distribution, and promotion of merchandising in connection with Project; and (3)
> all merchandising participations, royalties, or other fees paid to third parties."

i. In calculating MAGR the Network Subsidiary will impute a license fee

An imputed license fee is the amount that the Network Subsidiary receives in exchange for licensing the show to a company that either owns the Network Subsidiary or is owned by the Network Subsidiary. These amounts are artificial because they are not obtained in arm's length negotiations with unrelated third parties. If the Production Company has leverage, it will request that the Network Subsidiary add an "Exhibit" to the agreement containing terms that define what will constitute the imputed license fee. Some of the terms the Production Company would like to negotiate in the imputed license fee definition include: license fee, number of runs, platforms licensed, term, deficit recoupment formula, and ratings bonuses.

ii. Contingent Compensation hereunder shall vest fifty percent (50%) upon completion of Production Company's and Artist's services to the First Cycle and fifty percent (50%) upon completion of Production Company's and Artist's services to the Second Cycle;

The Production Company and Artist want their Contingent Compensation to vest 100%—that is, be irrevocably owned by them—immediately upon signing this Agreement. The Network Subsidiary would like to spread the percentage of vesting over a longer period of time so that if the Production Company or Artist stops providing their services to the show for any reason, then the Network Subsidiary will have those percentages of Contingent Compensation to offer to the subsequent production company and producer ("Artist"). The vesting schedule in the sample paragraph above are terms that are favorable to the Production Company and Artist—that is, it is more common for the percentages to vest over a greater number of cycles of the show.

The Network Subsidiary will also state that it makes no warranty, representation, or guarantee that the show will provide any gross receipts, any MAGR, or that any episode or episodes of the show will be produced, distributed, or exhibited.

(l) Series Lock. For clarity, Production Company and Artist shall be locked on a "pay-or-play" basis to provide production services on all episodes for the life of the Series, subject to all terms of this Agreement, including all Exhibits.

It is important for a production company and any individual providing services to the show to ask for and receive a "series lock" on a pay-or-play basis for the life of a show. If the Network Subsidiary agrees to these terms, then it is agreeing to provide the terms of this agreement (fees and credits are of particular interest to a production company and an individual providing services) so long as the show is being produced. Of course, the Network Subsidiary will want to add that the "series lock" is contingent on Production Company and Artist providing actual, in-person production services in accordance with the terms of this Agreement.

4. Approvals/Control.

The Production Company will commonly be responsible for the daily control over the physical production of the show. The Network Subsidiary usually demands approval over all creative, financial, and business decisions. Some of the aspects of the development and production that the network will demand control over include: the Pilot, the sales presentation reel, each budget, overages, producers, executive producers (most often specifying that the Artist is approved), writer(s), director(s), on-air talent (sometimes there will be a list of pre-approved on-air talent that is attached to the agreement as an Exhibit), any other company engaged as a subcontractor providing development or production services for the show, scripts, formats, music, and rough and final cut(s).

At the very least, a production company will want the network to agree to exercise its control rights "reasonably, in good faith, and in a timely manner so as to not interfere with the production company's delivery of an episode on time and on budget." Specific shows require negotiation and agreement regarding other areas of control such as the network's access to production locations, review of daily footage, rough cuts, final cuts, status reports to be provided by the production company, the production company's duty to promptly notify the network of any occurrence that may delay or preclude delivery of an episode, and other issues.

5. Advertising/Promotion/Marketing/Publicity.

The network commonly retains control over every aspect of advertising, promotion, marketing, and publicity for the show. They will require a production company, and all parties affiliated with it, to agree to not be involved in any of the advertising, promotion, marketing, and publicity unless directed by the network. The production company will want to obtain the right for incidental, non-derogatory, factually accurate, informational mention in their publicity, press notices, or other information with respect to their employment, the show, or the services to be rendered by them.

6. Product Placement and Brand Integration.

The network commonly retains control over every aspect of any and all product placement and integration, brand integration, sponsorship, advertising, and all other in-show promotions activities relating to the show. A production company will want to negotiate how "trade outs" will be applied. Companies may provide goods or services for free in exchange for integration of their brand in a show. One issue to negotiate is which party, the production company or the network, will determine the monetary value of such trade outs, because it is common that such amount is charged against the total line-item budget. Ideally, the production company wants to have the network agree that such trade out be only applicable against an appropriate line item of the budget based on money *actually received* in exchange from such trade out and not based on an assigned monetary value. Further, the production company will want to clarify that under no circumstances shall any product placement or brand integration be added to the "Gross Receipts" regarding the show, including, but not limited to, the network's calculation of MAGR.

7. Credits.

A production company and individuals providing services to the show will want to obtain the following on-screen credits: (1) the production company's logo (which is usually subject to the network's approval) on a separate card in the end titles on each episode of the show (the network will want to add that such credit is subject to the production company rendering and completing all required services); (2) "Executive Producer" credit for one (1) person to be designated by the production company (again, usually subject to the network's approval). The production company usually has more individuals that it has contractually agreed to provide such credits to, so it will need to obtain that number of credits from the network. The production company will want the credit to be on a separate card; the network will want it on a shared card. The production company will want such credit whether or not it renders services to a particular episode; the network will want to restrict it to only those episodes that the production company renders and for which it completes all required services.

The production company and individuals providing services will also need to negotiate and agree to the position, order, and duration on-screen that each credit will appear, in addition to the advertising in which the credits will appear. It is customary that the network will have the right to "squeeze" any and all credits regarding the show and any episode to enable promotional material or other material to be displayed on-screen simultaneously with credits.

8. No Obligation To Proceed.

A network makes it clear that it has no obligation to develop, order, produce, exhibit, release, perform, advertise, or distribute the show or make any use of the production services by the production company or any individual. This right is subject to any minimum orders that have been agreed to, any pay-or-play terms that have been agreed to, and any other guarantees that a network has agreed to in the agreement.

9. Takeover.

A network will have the right to give the production company directions and instructions to be followed by a production company or also simply take over the production or delivery of the show. These are extreme measures that a network is not eager to have to take, so the agreement commonly limits the circumstances in which the network can do this to some of the following: (1) If the projected cost of production of any episode of the show, in the network's good faith judgment, reasonably appears to exceed the applicable approved budget by 5% (excluding overage costs that are authorized in accordance with the terms of this Agreement, caused by *force majeure* or a direct consequence of a third party breach of contract that is not induced or encouraged by the production company). The production company wants to increase the percentage to 10% or even 15% in addition to including other items that will not be counted towards the aggregate amount of any budget overage; (2) if within three (3) business days a production company fails or refuses to perform in a reasonable time period any written request by a network to perform any material obligation of this agreement, including, but not limited to, production and delivery of the Pilot or any episode of the show; (3) if any petition under any bankruptcy or insolvency laws is filed by or against a production company; or (4) a production company is in breach, or the network believes, in its good faith judgment, that there is or will be a breach, of any of the material terms, conditions, representations, or warranties of this agreement. A production company will want to add that it be given notice of and a reasonable time to fix any breach or alleged breach.

If a network exercises these rights, the terms in this paragraph will also provide that the production company and any individuals have no further rights regarding the show but they are required to fully cooperate with the network to assist the network's efforts to produce and deliver the show on time and on budget, which shall include the requirement that the production company and all parties under contract with the production company continue to provide its services. Under such circumstances, the production company usually will be required to do so without compensation.

10. Grant of Rights. See Chapter 2.

Most often a reality show production services agreement will not have "reserved rights" under the Grant of Rights since it will be based on an original concept and the network will require complete ownership of all available rights. However, there are reserved rights if the show is based on a previously existing show, copyright, or trademark. For example, if a new show is based on an existing show in another country, then certain rights will already be subject to contractual obligations; or if a show is based on an existing trademarked property such as an operating business, then there can be merchandising, publishing, live event, and other rights that are not available for the network to acquire. For example, *American Choppers* reality show was based on the family owners of "Orange County Choppers," an existing custom and production motorcycle manufacturer. It would be wise for "Orange County Choppers" to reserve its right to continue to use and exploit the name of the company before, during, and after the reality show. If this became a "reserved right," the company would most likely be required to provide the network permission to use it in connection with the show. The terms of such use are subject to negotiation.

11. Security Interest.

The security interest required by a network is a function of the financing structure of reality television programs, and a brief description of the financing process is necessary to understand the importance of a security interest. The budget amount for a show is agreed upon and the network further agrees to provide the money for such budget. However, as evident in the paragraph "Series Services," the network does not immediately provide 100% of the cash for the production company to produce all of the required episodes. Instead, the network will provide a percentage of the cash at certain milestones in the development, production, and delivery of the show—for example, upon signing the agreement, upon commencement of pre-production, etc. Therefore, the production company is responsible to provide the funds necessary to fulfill its obligations until it is "reimbursed" by the network. It is possible that a production company has its own cash or line of credit to cover the expenses of the show until it is paid by the network. However, it is more likely that the production company will be required to obtain a loan from a bank, and the bank will require certain guarantees regarding the loan. One guarantee is literally a "guaranty" from the network that it will fulfill its obligations as provided in the agreement—that is, pay the production company. The terms of this "Guaranty" are commonly one to six pages in length and are attached as an exhibit to the agreement. Banks assess risk in deciding to provide a loan, and a guaranty from an established network is a factor that supports a bank's decision to provide these types of loans.

However, banks further reduce their risks involved in providing a loan by requiring the production company to provide the bank with a security interest in the show—that is, the bank will have a claim to the assets and revenue from the show if the loan is not repaid for any reason. The network also requires a security interest in the show if the production company doesn't fulfill its obligations, the terms of which are provided in this paragraph. The security interest granted to the network basically states that the network has a security interest in all of its right, title, and interest in and to the show. The precise definition of what is included in the "show" is open to interpretation, so the network will add a definition of what is included in its "right, title, and interest." This definition is called the "Collateral," which is commonly one to four pages in length and is attached as an exhibit to the agreement. For example, the Collateral definition will include the following language:

". . . Network's right, title, and interest in and to the Project, which, for the purposes hereof, shall mean the Concept, the Delivery Items, as more fully described in Exhibit __, the Series, and all elements thereof, copyrights, trademarks, patents, intellectual property, documents, goods, inventory, investment property, letter of credit rights, supporting obligations, accounts receivable, deposit accounts, contract rights and general intangibles, insurance proceeds, and claims . . . shall include the scenario, script (if applicable) upon which the project is based, all the properties thereof, tangible and intangible . . . The Project and all rights of every kind and nature (including, without limitation, copyrights) in and to all scenarios, teleplays, and/or scripts (including any and all drafts, versions, and variations) and any other literary, musical, dramatic, or other material of any kind or nature upon which, in whole or in part, the Project is or may be based . . . All physical properties of every kind or nature of or relating to the Project and all versions thereof . . . all physical elements of the Project, including all negatives, duplicate negatives, fine grain prints, soundtracks, positive prints (cutouts and trims excepted), and sound, all video formats (including PAL/NTSC) . . . all rights of every kind or nature in and to any and all music and musical compositions created for, used in or to be used in connection with the Project . . . "

As can been seen from above, a reality television show (as defined in this agreement, the Concept, Project, and Series) is comprised of a bundle of rights.

12. Unions and Guilds. See Chapter 2.

13. Assignment. See Chapter 2.

14. Confidentiality.

It is common for the network to require the production company and any individual providing services to agree to keep certain information confidential. It should be noted that most often the confidentiality clause is *not* mutual—that is, the network is not agreeing to keep information confidential.

The network will require the other parties to keep confidential information that includes the terms and conditions in the production services agreement in addition to any "proprietary information." Proprietary information is generally defined as: information that (a) is not known by actual or potential competitors of the network, (b) has been created, discovered, developed, or otherwise become known to the network, and (c) has material economic value or potential material economic value to the network's present or future business. Generally, it includes rights such as trade secrets, discoveries, developments, designs, improvements, inventions, formulas, software programs, processes, techniques, know-how, data, research, techniques, technical data, and customer and supplier lists. It may seem to be an over-reaching term to include proprietary information in a reality television agreement, but it is a common provision in contracts that are entered in states such as California. These states have strict limitations on one party's ability to stop another party from competing with it based on the parties' written agreement not to compete with each other after their relationship ends. However, one party, such as the network, could stop another party, the production company, from using any of the "proprietary information" it obtained during the relationship once the relationship ends.

There are limiting terms that the production company wants to add to these terms, such as the following: Confidential information shall not include information after it becomes available to or known by the general public other than as a result of disclosure by the production company. Proprietary information shall not include information that is independently developed by the production company without any use whatsoever of information provided by Network or is known to the production company at the time of disclosure by the Network. Further, the production company may disclose Confidential and Proprietary Information to its members, shareholders, partners, managers, directors, officers, employees, agents, representatives, consultants, investors ("Representatives"), and legal counsel ("Counsel"), to the limited extent they need to know such information. In addition, the production company may disclose Confidential and Proprietary Information to the extent required by applicable law (including by request for information or documents through legal proceedings, subpoena, governmental investigation, or any similar process) without liability and also may disclose the specific terms and conditions of this Agreement in order to enforce its rights pursuant to this Agreement.

16. Representations and Warranties. See Chapter 2.

17. Remedies.   See Chapter 2.

18. Miscellaneous.

In this paragraph the parties will identify the documents ("Exhibits") that are included with the Production Services Agreement, which commonly include the following: "Standard Terms and Conditions"; "Definition of Modified Adjusted Gross Receipts"; "Definition of Collateral"; "Guaranty Agreement"; and the "Delivery Requirements."

(A) **"Standard Terms and Conditions"** exhibit is between five and twenty-five pages in length. Networks have boilerplate terms and conditions that they add to most agreements they enter. It is stated at the beginning of the Standard Terms and Conditions that if there is a conflict between the terms and conditions of the Production Services Agreement and the terms in the Standard Terms and Conditions, then the Production Services Agreement terms shall control—that is, govern the outcome. Since it is boilerplate language, there are many topics and terms in this "Exhibit" that are duplicates of the terms found in the Production Services Agreement.

Topics found in the Standard Terms and Conditions that are often duplicative include: (1) Services To Be Provided; (2) Rights Granted; (3) Representations and Warranties; (4) Remedies; (5) No Obligation To Proceed; (6) Applicable Law; (7) Insurance; (8) Assignment; and (9) Unions and Guilds. These topics are covered in Chapter 2.

Areas covered in the Standard Terms and Conditions that are not often found in the body of the Production Services Agreement include: (1) Federal Communications Act: the production company will acknowledge that the Federal Communications Act makes it a criminal offense for any person, in connection with the production or preparation of any program intended for broadcasting, to accept or pay money, service, or other valuable consideration for the inclusion of any matter as a part of any such program without disclosing it. Further, the production company will agree not to accept or pay any such consideration, and it will not accept or pay, and has not paid nor will pay, any money, service, or other valuable consideration for the inclusion of any "plug," reference, or product identification, or of any other matter, in any program produced in connection with the Agreement. The network includes language that any party engaged in such actions shall be in breach of the Agreement and in "Default" (see below), which can result in dismissal and termination of the Agreement; (2) Morals: If at any time while an artist, production company, or anyone working for the production company commits any criminal offense or commits any act or is involved in any situation or occurrence that brings public scandal, disrepute, widespread contempt, public ridicule, or which is widely deemed by members of the general public to embarrass, offend, insult, or denigrate individuals or groups, or that will tend to shock, insult, or offend the community or public morals or decency or prejudice the Project, Series, or Concept, or licensee, sponsor, or advertising agency thereof, then the network shall have the right, in its sole discretion, to take any action it deems appropriate, including but not limited to terminating this Agreement, in addition to and without prejudice to any other remedy of any kind in its sole and unilateral judgment. Also see Chapter 2; (3) Work Permits and Visas: a production company is responsible to obtain and maintain all passports, visas, work permits, and immigration clearance of all those that are engaged by the production company; (4) Incapacity and Default: the circumstances under which the production company and any individual providing services to the network does not comply with the terms of the Agreement because of an incapacity or default are described, in addition to the network's remedies, which include termination of the Agreement; (5) Payments: the party who is to receive all payments and the method and timing of all payments is addressed in this paragraph; and (6) Accountings: If the network is responsible to account for future payments, then this paragraph provides how often, in what manner, and other terms applicable to accounting. The production company often will provide requested revisions to the terms of this paragraph to address such terms as the specific information required to be provided by the network in such accounting statements, the production company's rights to audit the books and records of the network, and the remedies the production company has if it is found that there is an underpayment by the network, including the right to have the network pay the production company's expenses to conduct the audit.

(B) **Definition of Modified Adjusted Gross Receipts** exhibit is between two and twenty pages in length. Whether it is a short version or a long version, the goal is to define what is included in "Gross Receipts," define what will be deducted from "Gross Receipts," which then identifies what amounts are "Modified Adjusted Gross Receipts" from which the production company will be paid a percentage (i.e., "Contingent Compensation"), see above.

Included in the items that are deducted from "Gross Receipts" are the following: (1) "Distribution Fees"; (2) "Distribution Expenses"; (3) "Production Costs"; (4) "Advances"; (5) "Deferments"; (6) "Interest"; and (7) "Third Party Participations." The network requires the production company and any individual providing services to acknowledge and agree that the network is a multi-national company that is a subsidiary of many parent companies, owns many subsidiary companies, and has the unilateral right to distribute and exploit the Project, Series, and Concept as, when, and where it decides in its own judgment with the latter "Affiliated Companies." These "Affiliated Companies" include wholly-owned and controlled exhibitors, networks, stations, programming services, "platforms," syndication and distribution companies, home video distributors, merchandising companies, video game companies, record companies, literary and electronic publishers, internet providers, internet companies, wholesale and retail sales outlets, and other companies involved in the distribution and exploitation of audiovisual works and related allied, ancillary, and subsidiary rights throughout the universe in all media now known or hereafter devised. Further, the production company and any individual providing services are required to acknowledge and agree to the following: (a) that such distribution and exploitation can and will be among these "Affiliated Companies"; (b) they expressly waive any right to object to the distribution and exploitation of the Project, Series, and Concept involving Affiliated Companies; and (c) they expressly waive the right to assert any claim that the network should have offered the distribution and exploitation of the Project, Series, and Concept to third-party, unaffiliated parties.

It is evident that the unilateral right of the network to essentially license the program's rights to itself provides the network the opportunity to manipulate the numbers to limit the amounts available to those parties who are required to receive "Contingent Compensation." The best a production company could hope to add to this language is that the network agrees that the terms agreed to between the network and Affiliated Companies will be reasonably consistent with the terms that those Affiliated Companies agreed to with unrelated third parties for comparable programs.

(C) **"Definition of Collateral"** is important to the "security interest" that the network claims in the Project, Series, and Concept. As stated above, this definition is between one and four pages in length with the goal to define all of the rights that are subject to the network's security interest.

(D) **"Guaranty Agreement"** is a statement by the network that it guarantees its prompt and complete performance of its obligations in the Production Services Agreement. Of primary importance is the network's promise to pay the funds as and when agreed upon by the parties. As explained above, the production company provides this signed guarantee to a lender that is often needed by the production company to cover the time between when it is required to produce the pilot or episodes of the show and the later date that the network promises to pay for delivery of the pilot or episodes.

(E) **"Delivery Requirements"** is an exhibit that is ten to twenty pages in length identifying every element that the production company is to provide to the network. The production company is required to provide the network the physical elements of production and the paperwork supporting the ownership and exploitation of the program. The requirements are detailed, which is another reason why networks most often work with production companies, producers, and legal counsel with experience producing and delivering a specific type of television programming. The physical delivery of the show to the network will contain terms that include: (1) the format; (2) video specifications such as the exact running time and the point at which color bars, audio tones, and other markers must be placed; (3) the number and types of videos to be delivered; (4) closed captioning; (5) credits, including placement and timing of logos; (6) the exact time each show must break for commercials; (7) on-air promotions requirements; (8) advertising and promotion requirements; (9) press and multi-platform requirements; (10) all paper documents for legal delivery, including, but not limited to: (a) all music cue sheets; (b) all legal documents obtaining all rights from all parties providing goods and services to the show; (c) detailed cost analysis; (d) cost analysis compared to the agreed upon budget; (e) final shooting schedule and comparison to the agreed upon shooting schedule; and many other required documents.

The production company and legal counsel carefully review all terms in the Delivery Requirements, revising the terms as needed. Payment from the network, in addition to avoiding claims of breach of the agreement by the network, are subject to the production company's careful and precise delivery of every item required by the network as detailed in this exhibit.

AGREED TO AND ACCEPTED:

PRODUCTION COMPANY   NETWORK SUBSIDIARY

By: _____   By: _____

Its: _____   Its: _____

DEAL POINT CHECKLIST
Production Services Agreement

1. Conditions Precedent
2. Development Services
   - All-Inclusive Fee
3. Series Services
   - Pilot
   - First Cycle
   - Project Options
     - Total Number of Options
     - Budget
     - Production Company and Artist Fees
     - Additional Cycles
   - Pilot and First Cycle Budgets
   - Overages/Underages
   - Production Duties
   - Clearances
   - Series Fee
   - Contingent Compensation
   - Series Lock
4. Approvals/Control
5. Advertising/Promotion/Marketing/Publicity
6. Product Placement and Brand Integration
7. Takeover
8. Standard Terms and Conditions

8

Location Agreement

1. **Rights.** The undersigned lessor ("_____") as owner of the premises described herein (or as agent for such owner) (hereinafter referred to as "Owner") irrevocably grants to Reality Television Productions, LLC, as lessee ("Producer"), and any agent, licensee, and/or assignee ("Successor") of Producer the right to use, access, and photograph (including without limitation by means of motion picture, still, or video device photography) both the real and personal property interior and exterior located at the premises generally described as follows:

_____

_____(the "Location")

It is important to describe the location in detail so there is no dispute during production regarding the Producer's right of access on the Location.

in any manner whatsoever in connection with the production of a reality television program tentatively entitled "Untitled Reality Program" (the "Show") including the right to photograph, record, and use any logos, trademarks, service marks, photographs, designs, sculptures, works, and verbiage and any signs contained on the premises, the right to refer to the premises or any part thereof by a fictitious name, and the right to attribute fictitious events as occurring on the premises.

There is often negotiation regarding what logos, trademarks, and other items described in this paragraph that a Producer can film and exploit. The Producer would like to have the right to film and exploit all of the rights that the Owner has, but the Owner is concerned about further payment regarding such uses and, perhaps, even more important to the Owner is the protection of the reputation and rights of a business that is represented by logos and trademarks that will be exploited in the show. For example, a show may concern a business and within the show, that business's name and logo may be portrayed in a way that is detrimental to the business owner. On the other hand, positive portrayal of the business would be good advertising for the show, so the Owner may want the Producer to film and exploit these rights.

Together with unencumbered access to and egress over said premises with Producer's personnel and equipment, for the purposes of erecting and maintaining temporary filming sets and structures, lighting and photographing of said premises, sets, and structures, and of recording sound for such work as Producer may desire.

The parties should negotiate and agree to which party is required to obtain any and all necessary permits for filming in the location. Usually it is the Producer's duty to obtain all permits.

If the show involves an ongoing business or any other activity that may involve the filming and/or participation of third parties, it is also usually the Producer's responsibility to obtain releases from all third parties in which they agree to be on camera and transfer to the Producer the right to use their name and likeness as well as other rights. It is a subject of negotiation if the Producer will film employees of a business, and the parties will identify those individuals who may be subject to a separate "Talent Agreement" (see Chapter 6) and other individuals who will only be incidentally involved in the show. The Producer will agree to conceal the identity of any individual who does not agree to sign a release to be filmed. In addition, the Producer will agree to place large, legible signs informing anyone from the public who enters that filming is in process and they are providing their release by entering. The latter requirement is usually a subject of clarification if the show involves a business, because the business will want to have control over the manner in which the show interacts with customers to avoid losing customers and earning negative feedback. The Producer does not want to give the business control over the production of the show, so the specific terms that are negotiated and agreed to will be based on the nature of the show and what the Producer will require to produce the show. If the business owner has enough leverage in the negotiations, it may be able to get the Producer to agree to certain control over the final episodes to be aired. (See "Control" in Paragraph 6 below).

2. **Right of Possession/Term.** Producer may take possession of said premises approximately _____ (time of day) on or about _____ (Date) and continuing until completion of all photographing and recording for which Producer may desire the use of said premises until approximately _____ (time of day) on or about _____ (Date).

The Producer will want to add that the date for taking possession of the premises is subject to change on account of weather conditions or changes in production schedule or any other contingency that is relevant. The Producer would like the ending period to continue until completion of all photographing and recording for which Producer may desire the use of the premises without adding an ending date. The Owner would prefer to have a definite end time agreed upon.

The Producer will want to negotiate and agree to an option to access the premises to film future "cycles" (seasons) of the show. The Producer would like the terms to be that the Producer has the option to access the premises on the same terms and conditions of this agreement, which the Producer can exercise in its sole and unilateral discretion within a reasonable time after the completion of the first "cycle" (season) of episodes. A reasonable time for the Producer to exercise this option is between thirty (30) and one hundred and eighty (180) days. The Owner would like the time period to be closer to the thirty (30) days and the Producer would like to have as much time as possible to make a decision. If the Producer exercises the option, then the parties are required to comply with the terms of this Agreement for a certain time period after the Owner receives notice of the Producer's exercise of the option. For example, the new time period can be defined as one (1) year after the exercise of the option or to continue from the date of the exercise of the option until completion of all photographing and recording for which Producer may desire the use of the Location.

The Producer will also want the Owner to agree that Producer has a number of exclusive, consecutive, and dependent options to extend the term after the first extension. At the least the Producer would want four (4) or five (5) options and the Owner would like to limit the number to one (1) or two (2).

The Producer will want the Owner to agree that during the Term (which includes any options exercised by the Producer) and for a reasonable time after the expiration of the Term that the Owner will not enter into any agreement with any third party concerning or regarding the production of any similar reality show. It is not uncommon for an exhibit to be attached to the agreement containing the treatment and one-sheet of the show to clarify what would be considered a "similar" show.

3. **Compensation.** Producer and Owner agree that Owner shall not be entitled to any compensation from any source whatsoever in connection with the subject matter of this Agreement and/or the use and exploitation of the Show.

It is possible for the Producer to obtain access to the premises without paying the Owner if the Owner is a business that values the exposure on a reality show as free advertising. However, more often the Owner of the Location is a party that is different than the owner of the businesses on the Location. Therefore, in these situations the Producer will need to negotiate a fee with the Owner for the right to film at the Location. Fees vary in accordance with the property to be accessed, the time period it is to be accessed, and the type of show the Producer is filming, among other factors.

4. **Re-entry.** At any time from the date Producer contemplates its use of said premises hereunder, Producer may, upon prior written notice to Owner and subject to Owner's approval, not to be unreasonably withheld, re-enter and use said premises for such period as may be reasonably necessary to photograph retakes, added scenes, and the like

desired by the Producer upon the same terms and conditions contained in the Agreement. The Producer may only re-enter and use said premises on another available date that has been reasonably scheduled by both parties.

> The Producer will want the right to re-enter the Location, but if the term that is agreed upon is a long term, for example, a year, then often the Owner will not want to grant this right to the Producer since the Owner will take the position that the term is long enough to complete the necessary filming. If the Owner refuses to grant this provision, the Producer would be wise to at least negotiate a daily rate that Producer can pay the Owner to be able to re-enter to film photograph retakes, added scenes, and the like.

5. **Ownership.** See Chapter 2.

> The Producer will want the agreement to clarify that all rights of every kind in and to all intellectual property created by Producer, including without limitation all photography, whether still or motion picture, and sound records made in connection with this Agreement shall be solely owned exclusively and in perpetuity by Producer, and not the Owner or any tenant or other party ever having an interest in the Location.
>
> It is also common for the Producer to add specific examples of the intellectual property such as all videotape in any format, all logos, trademarks, artwork, designs, and service marks.

6. **Control.**

> The Owner will acknowledge that the Producer has complete and unilateral control of the Show, including, but not limited to, absolute and final cutting authority with respect to the Show, and that the Producer will always have the right to otherwise modify, edit, add to, or delete from the Show as it may determine in its sole discretion.
>
> Sometimes a business or an Owner of the Location will require the right to review episodes before they are aired. The Producer will want to avoid having any control or editorial rights over the Show given to the Owner. The Owner's concerns can include the safety of its employees, the safety of the Location, protection of its brand name from

defamation, or being placed in a "false light" that could damage its reputation and economic rights.

If the Owner does obtain certain rights over the content of the Show, the parties will agree to a procedure and time frame in which the parties have to provide the episode for review, to provide feedback, to re-edit the Show, and then have a second review by the Owner. For example, the Owner could be provided seventy-two (72) hours to review an episode and provide feedback identifying any claims of defamatory or other damaging depictions of the business or Location. The Producer would then have a certain time period to re-edit the Show and provide the new version to the Owner. The Owner would then have a shorter period, perhaps a short as twenty-four (24) hours, to review and approve the changes. The language should also state that the Producer is obligated to alert the Owner to all changes that are contained in the revised version and also contain language regarding the procedure if the parties can't agree to whether or not the Producer has adequately addressed the Owner's concerns. For example, it could be that the Producer agrees to edit the content to extent of all reasonable demands by the Owner. On the other hand, the parties could agree that any dispute would be adjudicated by a neutral third party.

An Owner may also want to control activities that are conducted on the Location to ensure that it has control over any safety issues that may occur. If any safety issue arises, the Owner will want the right to stop the Producer from filming until the issue is resolved.

An Owner may also want to control any activities that interfere with the activities at a Location such as an ongoing business in addition to providing a list of rules and regulations that the Producer must follow when at the Location. The Owner will again want to stop the Producer from filming until any interference or violation of other rules or regulations is resolved.

7. Damages and Costs.

The Producer will agree to return the Location to its original condition. In return, the Producer will want the Owner to promise to deliver the Location in a clean condition with the existing electrical, plumbing, fire sprinkler, lighting, heating, ventilating and air conditioning systems, and all other relevant items in good operating condition. The Producer will also want the Owner to agree that return of the Location is subject to reasonable wear and tear.

The parties should also negotiate and agree which party will be responsible for payment of the cost of any maintenance and repair of the Location, or any equipment on the Location. The Producer will only want to be responsible for such costs to the extent they are attributable to abuse or misuse by the Producer.

The Producer will also want to have the right to park at the Location for no additional costs. If the Location is obtained for free, then the Producer will usually be responsible for any costs of parking at the Location in addition to the costs for the use of utilities, including the electricity, gas, water, and restrooms on the Location.

8. **No Actual Use.** Neither Producer nor its Successors shall be obligated to make any actual use of any photograph, recordings, depictions, or other references to the premises hereunder in any documentary motion picture or otherwise.

This clause is specifically important to discuss with the Owner if the Owner is providing access to the Location for free in exchange for anticipated benefits of exposure on television.

9. **Representations and Warranties. Indemnification.** See Chapter 2.
10. **Assignment.** See Chapter 2.
11. **Insurance.** See Chapter 2.

AGREED AND ACCEPTED BY:

_____ _____
("Producer")   ("Owner")

By: _____ By: _____

Its: _____ Its: _____

Date: _____ Date: _____

DEAL POINT CHECKLIST
Location Agreement

1. Rights
2. Right of Possession/Term
3. Compensation
4. Re-entry
5. Ownership
6. Control
7. Damages and Costs
8. No Actual Use
9. Representations and Warranties. Indemnification
10. Assignment
11. Insurance

Index

A

ABC, 6–7, 114, 136

Access to Locations (Consents and Authorizations), 86

Accountings, 170

Additional Cycle, 153–154

additional services, 119

Advances, 170

advertisers, 9–10

Advertising/Promotion/ Marketing/Publicity (Product Services Agreement), 163

Affiliated Companies, 170–171

On-Air Talent Agreement
  Ancillary Services Guarantee, 127–128
  Cast Insurance, 137–140
  Commercials/Promotional Episodes/Other Program Materials, 124–125
  Conditions Precedent, 104–105

Credit, 128–129

Deal Point Checklist, 143

Entire Agreement, 141–142

Exclusivity, 111–115

general information on, 102–103

Hair, Makeup and Wardrobe, 132

Merchandising, Ancillary Exploitation and Commercial Tie-Ins, 125–127

Miscellaneous, 141

Name, Likeness, Etc., 121–124

No Additional Compensation, 115–118

Promotion, 118–120

Publicity/Confidentiality, 135–137

Series Rules, 132–133

Series Services, 105–110

In–Show Integrations, 120–121
Standards of Performance;
    Consultation Rights,
    133–134
Travel and Expenses,
    130–132
On-air talent agreements, 10
The Amazing Race, 6–7, 136
Amazing Race, 40
The American Arbitration
    Association (AAA), 21
An American Family, 5, 6
American Idol, 6–7, 114, 150
America's Got Talent, 7
America's Next Top Model, 20, 99
America's Top Model, 7
Amy's Baking Company, 99
Ancillary Services Guarantee
    (On-Air Talent Agreement),
    127–128
Ancillary Use, 114
Applicable Law/Venue, 20
Applicant/Participant/Release
    agreement, 69–70
Application, 70–71, 87–88
The Apprentice, 6, 7
Approvals (Talent Attachment
    Agreement), 39, 41–42
Approvals/Controls (Production
    Services Agreement), 162
Arbitration, 20–21
Artist's Credit, 38–39
Artist's Exclusivity, 38

Artist's Fee, 38
Assignment, 15
Assumption of Risk, 91–93
Assumption of Risk / Hazardous
    Activity, 138–139
Attaching Artist and
    Artist's Business
    Compensation, 34
    Exclusivity, 37
    Representations and
        Warranties, 44
    Results and Proceeds/Grant
        of Rights/Rights, 40
    Services, 31–32
Attaching Artist and Artist's
    Family (or group), 34–35

B
The Bachelor, 99
Bachelor/Bachelorette, 136–137
Bar Rescue, 147
BBC, 137
Big Brother, 6–7, 69
The Biggest Loser, 6, 7, 20
Binding Agreements
    (Talent Attachment
    Agreement), 45
boilerplate terms
    Applicable Law/Venue, 20
    Arbitration, 20–21
    Assignment, 15
    Breach and Incapacity, 16–17
    definition of, 11–12

Force Majeure, 17–178
Indemnification, 14–15
Insurance, 19
Morals, 18–19
Non-Guild Agreement, 20
Remedies, 15–16
Representations and
    Warranties, 13–14
Results and Proceeds/Grant
    of Rights/Rights, 12–13
Breach and Incapacity, 16–17
Bunim/Murray Productions, 9

C
Candid Camera, 5
Carbone, Steve "Reality," 137
"carve out," 36–37
Cast Insurance (On-Air Talent
    Agreement), 137–140
CBS, 6–7, 9, 58, 136
CMT, 145
Collaboration Agreement
    clarification of parties
        involved, 50–51
    Deal Point Checklist, 66
    definition of, 49–50
    Disposition of the Project,
        53–59
    interest in a product, 9
    Term of Agreement, 51–53
Collateral, 166–167, 171
Commercials and
    Endorsements, 115

Commercials/Promotional
    Episodes/Other Program
    Materials (On-Air Talent
    Agreement), 124–125
Compensation
    On-Air Talent Agreement, 108
    Location Agreement, 177–178
    Talent Hold/Option, 33–34
Conditions Precedent
    On-Air Talent Agreement,
        104–105
    Production Services
        Agreement, 147–148
    Talent Attachment
        Agreement, 28–29
Confidential and Proprietary
    Information, 168
Confidential Information, 97
Confidentiality
    Participant Agreement, 97–100
    Production Services
        Agreement, 167–168
Consents and Authorizations
    Access to Locations, 86
    Assumption of Risk, 91–93
    Confidentiality, 97–100
    Grant of Rights, 88–89
    Life Story Rights, 89–91
    Participant Agreement, 85–87
    Participant Application, 87–88
    Permitted Items, 86
    Physical health, 85–86
    Privacy Waivers, 86

Releases and Waivers, 93–101
Contingent Compensation, 138, 170
contract language. *See* boilerplate terms
Control (Location Agreement), 178–179
Cops, 6
Credit (On-Air Talent Agreement), 128–129
Credits (Product Services Agreement), 164
Cycle Option, 152–153

D
Damages and Costs (Location Agreement), 179–180
Dancing with the Stars, 10, 40
Dancing With the Stars, 7
Deadliest Catch, 70, 147
Deal Point Checklist
    On-Air Talent Agreement, 143–144
    Collaboration Agreement, 66
    information on, 10
    Location Agreement, 181
    Production Services Agreement, 173
    Talent Attachment Agreement, 46
defamatory actions, 80
Deferments, 170

Definition of Modified Adjusted Gross Receipts, 170
Delivery Requirements, 156, 172
Developmental Services (Production Services Agreement), 148
discontinuing participation (quitting the series), 76–78
Disposition of the Project (Collaboration Agreement)
    Approvals/Controls, 59–61
    Binding Agreements, 64
    Expenses, 61
    Miscellaneous, 64
    Net Profits, 56–57
    pilots, specials and/or series, 54–56
    Project Ownership, 57–59
    Reversion, 62–64
Distribution Expenses, 170
Distribution Fees, 170
Duck Dynasty, 7, 70, 73
DVD Copies, 139

E
E! News, 114
Early, Jim, 99
episode summaries, 7–9
Episodic Fees, 106–109
equitable remedies, 15
Exclusive Hold Period, 74–75

Exclusivity (On-Air Talent Agreement), 111–115

Exclusivity (Talent Attachment Agreement), 35–36

Executive Producer credit, 164

Extreme Weight Loss, 147

Eyeworks, 9

F

Face the Nation, 6

Family, 5

Fast N' Loud, 147

Fear Factor, 69, 92

Federal Communications Act, 169

Federal Communications Act (On-Air Talent Agreement), 134–135

51 Minds, 9

Filming Artist's Children, 138

First Cycle Budget, 155

first priority basis, 158

First Series Option, 105

Force Majeure, 17–18

Fox, 6–7, 114

G

goals of the book, 1–2

Grant of Rights, 12–13
Participant Agreement, 88–89

Production Services Agreement, 165–166

Gross Receipts, 170

Guaranty Agreement, 171

H

Hair, Makeup and Wardrobe (On-Air Talent Agreement), 132

Hantz, Russell, 99

HaperCollins, 137

Hatch, Richard, 88

Hell's Kitchen, 7

Hidden Camera, 138

I

ideas, legal protection of, 8

ideas for reality shows, 25

Incapacity and Default, 170

Indemnification, 14–15

INS Form I-9 (Employment Eligibility Verification), 104

Insurance, 19

Interest, 170

Introduction/Application (Participant Agreement), 70–73

J

JAMS (formerly Judicial Arbitration and Mediation Services), 21

Jeopardy, 40
The Jersey Shore, 10
Jersey Shore, 7, 70, 73, 82,
    88–89, 160
Jon and Kate Plus 8, 7
Judge Judy, 40

K
Keeping Up With The Kardashians,
    6, 7, 25
Kitchen Nightmares, 99
Klum, Heidi, 132
Knock Before Entering, 138

L
Last Comic Standing, 7
legal disclaimer, 2
leverage and lack of, 9–10
Life Story Rights, 89–92
Little Couple, 6
Location Agreement
    Compensation, 177
    Control, 178–179
    Damages and Costs, 179–180
    No Actual Use, 180
    Ownership, 178
    Right of Possession/Term,
        176–177
    Rights, 174–176
Location Fee, 138
log-lines, 7–9

M
Medical considerations
    (Consents and
    Authorizations), 86–87
Merchandising, Ancillary
    Exploitation and
    Commercial Tie-Ins
    (On-Air Talent), 125–127
Merchandising Revenue
    (MR), 160
The Million Second Quiz, 114
The Millionaire Matchmaker, 150
Mixology, 114
Modified Adjusted Gross
    Receipts (MAGR), 160–161,
    163, 170
Morals, 18–19, 169–170
most favored nations, 160
MTV, 145
Mutual of Omaha's Wild
    Kingdom, 5

N
Name, and Likeness (On-Air
    Talent Agreement), 121–124
Name/Likeness/Biography
    (Talent Attachment
    Agreement), 41–42
NBC, 6–7, 9, 58, 114
network examples, 9
network production services
    agreement (PSA). *See*

PSA (network production
services agreement)
Network Subsidiary, 145–146
Nickelodeon, 145
No Actual Use (Location
Agreement), 180
No Additional Compensation
(On-Air Talent Agreement),
115–118
No Coast Originals, 147
No Obligation to Proceed
(Product Services
Agreement), 164
Non-Disclosure Agreement,
97–100
Non-Guild Agreement, 20
Non-Union, 20
Non-Union (Talent Attachment
Agreement), 40
Nudity, 139
NZK Productions and Horizon
Alternative Television, 137

O
one-sheet, 7–9
Option, 29
Option Artist, 31
Option Period, 29, 35
Original Productions, 147
The Osbournes, 6
other parties, 94
Ownership (Location
Agreement), 178

P
Participant Agreement
Consents and Authorizations,
85–87
Introduction/Application,
70–73
Participation and
Acknowledgements,
73–84
Rules, 84–85
participant agreement, 10
Participant Application, 87–88
participants, 10
Participation and
Acknowledgements, 73–84
Participation and
Acknowledgements
(Participant Agreement),
73–84
Party Down South, 70
pay or play, 162
Payments, 170
"pay-or-play," 108
"people who write the checks," 9
Permitted Items (Consents and
Authorizations), 86–87
Physical health (Consents and
Authorizations), 85–86
Pilgrim Studios, 9
Pilot, 148–149
Pilot Budget, 155
Pilot Fees, 148–149
players, 8–9

post production services, 117
pre-production services, 116–117
The Price Is Right, 6
privacy, 78–80
Privacy Waivers (Consents and
    Authorizations), 86
Producer Credit / Separate
    Line-Item for Producing
    Services, 138
producer roles, 8–10
Product Placement and Brand
    Integration (Product
    Services Agreement), 163
Product Services Agreement
    Grant of Rights, 165–166
    Takeover, 164–165
Production Bonus, 159
production companies, 9
Production Costs, 170
Production Duties (Product
    Services Agreement),
    157–158
Production of the Program
    (Talent Attachment
    Agreement), 37–38
Production Services Agreement
    Advertising/Promotion/
        Marketing/Publicity, 163
    Approvals/Controls, 162
    Conditions Precedent,
        147–148

Confidentiality, 167–168
Credits, 163–164
Developmental Services, 148
information on and
    introduction to, 145–146
Miscellaneous, 169–172
No Obligation to Proceed,
    164
Product Placement and
    Brand Integration, 163
Security Interest, 166–167
Series Services, 148–162
production services agreement,
    9, 11
Project Ownership
    (Collaboration Agreement)
    Episodic Fees, 58–59
    Good Faith Negotiation, 59
    Level of Services, 58
    Travel, 59
Project Ownership (Talent
    Attachment Agreement),
    42–44
Project Runway, 89, 132
Project with Artist, 29
Promotion, 118–120
PSA (network production
    services agreement), 102
Publicity/Confidentiality
    (On-Air Talent Agreement),
    135–137

Q

Queen for a Day, 5
Quiz Show, 133

R

Ratings Bonus, 159–160
Ratings Bonus / Production
    Bonus, 138
*The Real Housewives of New
    Jersey*, 99
The Real Housewives of New York,
    34
Real Housewives of New York, 70
*The Real Housewives of Orange
    County*, 30
The Real Housewives (series),
    7, 25
The Real World, 6, 7, 69, 82
reality television
    development of, 7–9
    genres of, 6
    history of, 5–7
    legal protection of ideas, 8
    players of, 8–10
released parties, 95
Releases and Waivers, 93–101
Representations and Warranties,
    13–14
Representations and Warranties
    (Talent Attachment
    Agreement), 44
representing production
    companies, 47–48

Restaurant: Impossible, 6
Results and Proceeds/Grant of
    Rights/Rights, 12–13
Results and Proceeds/Grant
    of Rights/Rights (Talent
    Attachment Agreement), 40
Rich Kids of Instagram, 25
right, title, and interest, 166
Right of Possession/Term
    (Location Agreement),
    176–177
Rights (Location Agreement),
    174–176
Rob Dyrdek's Fantasy Factory, 25
Rules (Participant Agreement),
    84–85

S

SAG-AFTRA, 38, 40, 117, 129,
    131
Salvage City, 147
Seacrest, Ryan, 114
season structure, 7–9
Security for Personal
    Appearances, 138
Security Interest (Product
    Services Agreement),
    166–167
Series Lock, 162
Series Options (Talent Attachment
    Agreement), 32–33
Series Rules (On-Air Talent
    Agreement), 132–133

Series Services (On-Air
  Talent Agreement)
  First Series Year, 105–108
  Second and Subsequent
    Series Years, 109–110
Series Services (Production
  Services Agreement)
  Budget, 154–155
  Clearances, 158–159
  Contingent Compensation,
    160–161
  First Cycle, 149–150
  other services and monthly
    cost reports, 155
  Overages/Underages,
    155–156
  Pilot, 148–149
  Production Duties, 157–158
  Project Options, 150–154
  Series Fee, 159–160
  Series Lock, 162
series year, 108
serious actionable invasion of
  privacy, 78–79
Services (Talent Attachment
  Agreement), 31
Seven Up, 5
Shahs of Sunset, 20, 114
Shed Media, 9
shopping (developing and
  submitting project), 26
shopping agreement, 9, 11

In-Show Integrations (On-Air
  Talent Agreement), 120–121
sizzle reel, 146, 148–149
Skinnygirl Margarita, 34
So You Think You Can Dance, 89
Sorrention, Mike "The
  Situation," 88–89
Standard Terms and Conditions,
  169
Standards of Performance;
  Consultation Rights (On-Air
  Talent Agreement), 133–134
Stillman, Stacy, 136–137
Storage Wars, 147
Subsequent Series Year Option, 109
Survivor, 5, 6–7, 20, 38, 69, 88,
  99, 136–137
Survivor Entertainment Group,
  136–137

T
T Group Productions, 9
Takeover (Product Services
  Agreement), 164–165
Talent Attachment Agreement
  Approvals, 39
  Attaching Artist and Artist's
    Business, 31–32, 34–35,
    37, 40
  Binding Agreements, 45
  Compensation, 33–34
  Conditions Precedent,
    28–29

Deal Point Checklist, 46
definition of, 8–9
example of: "Untitled
    Reality Project," 27–28
Exclusivity, 35–36
importance of, 25–27
Miscellaneous, 45
Name/Likeness/Biography,
    41–42
Non-Union, 40
Production of the Program,
    37–38
Project Ownership, 42–44
Representations and
    Warranties, 44
Results and Proceeds/Grant
    of Rights/Rights, 40
Series Option, 32–33
Services, 31
Talent Hold/Option, 29–31
Talent Hold/Option (Talent
    Attachment Agreement),
    29–31
Television Critics Association
    (TCA) Press Tour, 117
television packages (representing
    production companies),
    47–48
Term of Agreement
    (Collaboration Agreement),
    51–53
Third Party Participants, 170
3 Ball Entertainment, 147

Top Chef, 36
Top Gear, 137
treatments, 7–9

U

Ultimate Women's Challenge, 137
*The Undersea World of Jacques
    Cousteau*, 5
unions and reality shows, 20
United States Copyright Office, 8
Untitled Reality Project
    (ex. Talent Attachment
    Agreement), 27–45
Untitled Reality Show
    (Collaboration Agreement),
    49–65

V

Viacom, Inc., 145–146
Viacom Media Networks,
    145–146
The View, 6

W

Warner Bros., 137
Who Wants to Be a Millionaire,
    47–48
William Morris Endeavor, 48
withdrawing from the series
    (agreements for), 76–78
Work Permits and Visas, 170
work-for-hire, 11
The Wrap (website), 48

Books from Allworth Press

Allworth Press is an imprint of Skyhorse Publishing, Inc. Selected titles are listed below.

Hollywood Dealmaking: Negotiating Talent Agreements for Film, TV and New Media
by Dina Appleton and Daniel Yankelevits (paperback, 6 x 9, 320 pages, $24.95)

Independent Film Producing: How to Produce a Low-Budget Feature Film
by Paul Battista (paperback, 6 x 9, 312 pages, $19.95)

Your Child's Career in Music and Entertainment: The Prudent Parent's Guide from Start to Stardom
by Steven C. Beer with Kathryne Badura (paperback, 5 ½ x 8 ¼, 176, $14.99)

The Health & Safety Guide for Film, TV & Theater
by Monona Rossol (paperback, 6 x 9, 256 pages, $19.95)

Technical Film and TV for Nontechnical People
by Drew Campbell (6 x 9, 256 pages, paperback, $24.95)

Career Solutions for Creative People
by Dr. Ronda Ormont (6 x 9, 320 pages, paperback, $27.50)

The Directors: Take Four
by Robert J. Emery (6 x 9, 256 pages, paperback, $22.95)

Documentary Superstars
By Marsha McCreadie (6 x 9, 256 pages, paperback, $19.95)

Managing Artists in Pop Music: What Every Artist and Manager Must Know to Succeed
by Mitch Weiss and Perri Gaffney (paperback, 6 x 9, 288 pages, $23.95)

Mastering Monologues and Acting Sides: How to Audition Successfully for Both Traditional and New Media
by Janet Wilcox (paperback, 6 x 9, 256 pages, $29.95)

Starting Your Career as an Actor
by Jason Pugatch (paperback, 6 x 9, 320 pages, $19.95)

Starting Your Career in Voice-Overs
by Talon Beeson (paperback, 6 x 9, 208 pages, $16.95)

To see our complete catalog or to order online, please visit *www.allworth.com*.